CAPITAL STRUCTURE
AND
CORPORATE CONTROL

CAPITAL STRUCTURE AND CORPORATE CONTROL

By

Ranjul Rastogi

Lecturer in Economics

Amity Law School, Delhi

ANMOL PUBLICATIONS PVT. LTD.

NEW DELHI - 110 002 (INDIA)

ANMOL PUBLICATIONS PVT. LTD.
4374/4B, Ansari Road, Daryaganj
New Delhi - 110 002

Capital Structure and Corporate Control

First Edition, 2001

ISBN 81-261-0727-8

ICSSR Consultant: Dr. R.K. Mishra

[The publication of this book is partially financed by the Indian Council of Social Science Research, New Delhi. However, the responsibility for the facts stated, conclusion reached etc., is entirely that of the Author and the ICSSR bears no responsibility for them.]

PRINTED IN INDIA

Published by J.L. Kumar for Anmol Publications Pvt. Ltd., New Delhi - 110 002 and Printed at Mehra Offset Press, Delhi.

Dedicated
To My Teacher
Prof. T.V.S. Ramamohan Rao

Preface

The modern corporation differs from the neoclassical characterization in two basic respects: (a) largeness and diffused ownership under limited liability, and (b) delegation of decision making power. Both these aspects have implications for the (a) locus of control with respect to long term decisions, and (b) objectives of control.

Three types of control systems have been acknowledged in the financial economics and financial management: (a) market for corporate control, (b) the governance mechanism, and (c) the implicit contract. Recent empirical studies demonstrated the inefficiency of the market for corporate control in an environment where there is diffused shareholding. Consequently, most of the firms supplement it by one of the other control structures.

In general, the shareholders have control rights regarding decisions, but the lack of information, the private cost of exercising control, and the delegation of decision making shift effective control from the shareholders to the board of directors. In such a system, the management is expected to implement the decisions made by the board. Williamson labels this control system as the governance mechanism. However, the information requirements and the frequency of strategic decisions may convince the board of directors that delegation to the management in an implicit contract will be more efficient. The board of directors devises some monitoring and incentive schemes to ensure bonding. Both these control systems are subject to adverse selection and moral hazard in the sense that there will be some discretionary use of resources. As such the shareholders will be compelled to accept some reduction in the market value of the firm to ensure that the implicit contract or the governance mechanism is sustainable at an efficient level albeit a second best.

A direct test of the prevalence of one of these organizational structures over the other would necessitate (i) estimating the several cost components associated with each of these decisions, and (ii) their relative valuation by the shareholders and the management. Both these approaches involve additional costs to the firm.

The theoretical arguments have not been sufficient to provide guidelines for a specific choice in a given empirical context. As of now, the available evidences are at best fragmentary. As Yarrow (1973, and 1976, p.267) stated the fundamental problem, "once managerial discretion is allowed, economic theory can have little to say about the components and shapes of managerial utility functions."

From the empirical perspective, as Lintner (1971, p. 218) remarked, the knowledge regarding managerial preferences remained incomplete since it has not been possible to estimate the relative weights which the management assigns to value increasing objectives and other aspects which they take into account. Schmalensee (1989, p. 957), Radice (1971, p. 549), and Cubbin and Leech (1986, p. 124) recognized the existence of an identification problem that can not be handled by the commonly employed estimation techniques and must be resolved. There has been a very limited progress on the empirical front as a result of these fundamental conceptual difficulties.

With these arguments in perspective the present study attempts to examine the following three aspects of the problem: (a) An attempt will be made to identify the locus of control of any given firm, and the reasons for the specific choice, (b) A modelling exercise will be developed to determine the direction and extent of managerial discretion in the context of a specific firm. The two major theoretical contributions concerning the corporate control and capital structure decisions, viz., the Marris (1964) model and the bonding hypothesis of Grossman and Hart (1982) should be kept in perspective. The models should also describe the channels through which incentives and constraints modify managerial behavior. A simple estimation method will be developed for the resolution of identification problem. (c) Detailed empirical estimates for several firms in the chemical industry will be developed to provide insights into the managerial decision making process at work.

On the whole, this study is a first step, albeit an important one, to make fundamental progress in the area of corporate control and strategic financial decisions of modern corporations.

Delhi

Ranjul Rastogi

Acknowledgements

Though words are imperfect to express the gratitude, I wish to express my gratitude and indebtedness to my Ph.D. Supervisor Prof. T.V.S. Ramamohan Rao for all the encouragement, meticulous care and affection he has shown towards me during the course of this work. I am grateful to Prof. R.R. Barthwal for his valuable comments and suggestions and Dheeraj for his practical insights into the problem.

My sincere thanks to Dr. Ashok Kumar Chauhan, President, Ritnand Balved Education Foundation and Prof. M.K. Balachandran, Director, Amity Law school, Delhi for their constant encouragement and support.

Part of this work has been presented at various seminars and published in journals. I appreciate the scholars' comments and suggestions which helped me in rethinking the specific issues.

I am grateful to Indian Council of Social Science Research for the financial assistance which they provided for the publication of this work. However the views expressed here are entirely those of the author and the ICSSR is in no way responsible for the contents.

I am also thankful to Anmol Publication Pvt. Ltd. for the bringing out this publication efficiently and timely.

As always, without the constant and cheerful support and patience of my parents, brother & sisters and brothers-in-law I would not have succeeded in completing my work.

Delhi

Ranjul Rastogi

Contents

List of Tables

List of Figures

List of Variables

S.No.	*Variable*	*Label*
1.	Market value of the firm	MAVA or V
2.	Debt equity ratio	DEBT or θ
3.	Rate of growth of capital assets	GRTH or g
4.	Net sales	NSAL
5.	Business risk	BSRI
6.	Financial risk	FIRI
7.	Inventory to sales ratio	INSA
8.	Capacity utilization	CAPA
9.	Net profit	NPRO
10.	Liqiudity ratio	LIQD
11.	Taxation rate	TAXT
12.	Wages and salaries to cost of goods sold	WASA
13.	Dividends per share	DIND

1

Introduction

1.1 Control in a Modern Corporation

The activities of every firm consist of the following:

(a) acquiring human and physical capital, and material resources,

(b) obtaining adequate finance,

(c) organizing production, and

(d) recovering money by selling the outputs.

The control (decision making) function relates to

(a) determining the appropriate quantity of resources and the timing of their acquisition, and

(b) ensuring their efficient use in production.

The neoclassical theory of the firm assumes that the owner manager

(a) makes all the decisions,

(b) bears the risks, and

(c) claims the residual rewards.

Within the framework of this theory two aspects of the control should be noted:

(a) In their efforts to reduce the impact of business risk[1] the firms make an attempt to exploit (i) the economies of scale and scope (which result from technological and/or organizational synergies) in a given product line and thereby obtain some market power, and/or (ii) the advantages of a diversified product range which can provide a cost reduction and/or stabilize the market share. Consequently, each firm attempts to (i) anticipate the emerging market trends ahead of others, and (ii) identify profitable investments and implement them efficiently. See, for instance, Fillipi and Zanetti (1971, p.147), and Lintner (1971, p.172).

(b) Control is centralized in the hands of the owner manager. It is therefore expected that the (i) short run goal of profit maximization, and (ii) long run objective of maximizing the market value of the capital assets of the firm will be pursued efficiently.

The modern corporation operates in an environment which differs from the neoclassical characterization in two basic respects:

(a) the firms are typically large and diffused ownership under limited liability becomes a necessity since no one person can finance all the activities, and
(b) the largeness of size necessitates a delegation of decision making in a complex organizational set up.

Both these aspects have implications for the

(a) nature of control,
(b) locus of control, and
(c) objectives of control.

It would be useful to elaborate on each of these aspects briefly.

A large size of capital assets is a necessary concomitant

of a strategy of product diversification. The largeness of size, in its turn, necessitates substantial amounts of finance to undertake capital investments. Hence, no one individual would be (i) able to finance the entire physical capital of the firm,and (ii) willing to bear all the losses in case of failure. Diffused shareholding, with its implications of limited liability, emerges in response to the need to share the risks. One of the consequences of this arrangement is that anyone of the shareholders

(a) is unlikely to have the information or the expertise[2] to manage the firm efficiently, and

(b) may, as Berle and Means (1932) argued, prefer to free ride on the decisions of the others since the private benefits may not be commensurate with the costs of undertaking the monitoring.

Diffused shareholding necessitates some modifications in the concept of corporate control. The following aspects are representative:

(a) Berle and Means (1932, p.69) emphasized the power to select the board of directors as the crucial aspect of corporate control.

(b) Leech and Leahy (1991) also include the power to exercise discretion over major decision making.

Such controlling power, as Cubbin and Leech (1983) put it, may ultimately depend on securing a simple majority vote in a meeting of the shareholders.

Efficient management of such enterprises also necessitates a complex organizational structure. In particular, there is a necessity for an efficient mechanism for the allocation of the capital assets of the firm to different activities on the basis of their long run strategic importance. However, as in the case of the financial arrangements

(a) no single person within the firm has the requisite information or expertise, and

(b) it may be expensive to achieve efficient monitoring and control if authority is vested in one person.

Stated in broad general terms the information requirements of large size necessitate an elaborate organizational arrangement to achieve efficient coordination.

The concept of corporate control should therefore include "the management of corporate resources - that is, the right to hire, fire, and set the compensation to the top level management." See, for instance, Fama and Jensen (1983).

In sum, in the context of a modern corporation, the concept of corporate control should encompass both the strategic and operating decisions.

Consider the locus of control. In general, as Fama (1990, p.S78) and Hill and Jones (1992) pointed out, equity contracts usually contain the provision that the rights of control regarding the decisions that affect the net cashflows are largely in the realm of the equity holders since they bear all the residual risk. However,

(a) the lack of information,

(b) the private cost of exercising control, and

(c) the delegation of decision making

shift effective control to the board of directors chosen by the shareholders. In turn, the board of directors may find it necessary to delegate decision making to the management who have the information advantage and retain a supervisory role especially with respect to strategic decisions. As a result, the choice of the financial instruments, in particular, the debt equity ratio and delegation of decision making to the divisional managers reduce the control of the board of directors. The effective control of corporate decisions passes to the management.

To the extent the board of directors retains the control they endeavor to define incentives (in the form of compensation schemes) and constraints (such as dividend payments) to entice the management to make decisions in consonance with the objectives of the shareholders. On the other hand, the management exercises control to achieve their objectives even if the shareholders' goals are compromised to a certain extent. Fundamentally, the control loss, from the perspective of fulfilling shareholders' preference, is intrinsic to the functioning of such firms.

1.2 The Nature and Role of Control Systems

The fundamental premise of the theories of corporate control is that there is a need for an efficient control system[3] even if the product and capital markets are static and not subject to environmental uncertainty. As McInnes and Carlton (1982, pp.960ff), and Williamson (1983, p.357) pointed out, the control systems should be such that they can

(a) provide the decision makers the requisite information regarding the nature, extent, and frequency of business risk,
(b) generate efficient decisions after taking the changing market conditions and the interaction of the product and financial markets into account, and
(c) define and implement an efficient resolution of the goal conflict between the shareholders and the management.

Three types of control systems have been considered in the literature:

(a) the capital market and the external control that it provides,
(b) a centralized decision process in the hands of the board of directors, and
(c) an implicit contract with the management with a supervisory role assigned to the board of directors.

As noted in the previous section the shareholders, as owners of the modern corporation, delegate certain control rights to

(a) the board of directors, and/or
(b) the management teams within the firm.

The justification for this choice is the reduction in the transaction costs of conducting the decisions through the market as noted by Coase (1937), and/or the agency costs alluded to by Jensen and Meckling (1976). However, as both these studies noted, the shareholders can revert to the market mode of control if the alternatives are inefficient. That is, as Klein and Leffler (1981) pointed out, the market can play the conditioning role in the functioning of contractual obligations.

Consider the pertinent aspects of these control systems briefly. It is generally surmised that the market for corporate control (via the takover threat) can achieve the desired coordination. As Jensen and Ruback (1983, p.6) pointed out, "competition among managerial teams for the rights to manage resources limits divergence from shareholders' wealth maximization by the managers and provide the mechanism through which economies of scale or the other synergies available from combining or reorganizing control and management of corporate resources are realized." Also see p.23. However, it has been demonstrated in recent empirical studies that the external control via the capital market is inefficient[4] and affords considerable scope for managerial discretion. See, for instance, Kaysen (1959, p.90), Jensen and Ruback (1983, p.29), Stultz (1988), and Smith and Watts (1992).

Consequently, the shareholders, or the board of directors as their representatives, consider it necessary to define firm specific control structures to maximize the market value of the firm. They generally complement the control offered by the capital market.

One alternative available to the board of directors is to retain control. Williamson (1988) labels this control system as the governance mechanism. In this form of control the board of directors

(a) examines the alternatives, especially of long term strategic nature, and

(b) makes the decisions which the management will be expected to implement.

Fundamentally this resembles the functioning of an internal capital market[5]. It becomes a necessary supplement to the operation of the external capital market.

However, in practice, the M-Form organization is the only context in which the governance mechanism has been examined in detail. The survey of the pertinent literature by Cable (1988) indicates that there are various inefficiencies and costs involved in its operation. In particular,

(a) Cable (1988, p.20) argued convincingly that, "profit maximizing behavior at the top level remains only an assumption underlying the M-Form hypothesis, and perhaps its strongest assumption." Instead, many authors, including Williamson (1971, p.380), Chandler (1977, p.10), and Stephen and Thompson (1988, p.180), noted the possibility that the staff at the headquarters prefers to pursue growth of capital assets and/or the stability of the market share in preference to profit and value maximization.

(b) as Cable (1988) noted, there is always a possibility that the information available at the headquarters to make an efficient capital allocation as well as reduce the moral hazard (opportunism of the management) would be inadequate. That is, as Cable (1988, p.20) put it, "the desirable control properties of the M-Form in constraining lower

> level behavior towards an overall objective, and avoiding organizational chaos after rapid and diversified expansion cannot be taken for granted."

On the whole, while there is inadequate empirical evidence on the efficiency of the governance mechanism, there are indications that its operation will not be fully in consonance with the objectives of the shareholders if they are stated in terms of the maximization of the market value of the capital assets of the firm.

The board of directors may resort to an implicit contract as the superior organizational choice. This organizational arrangement postulates that the shareholders invest their money in the capital assets of the firm and entrust the strategic decisions to the management. Such an organizational arrangement has the potential of entrusting various decisions to the individuals who have the best information. As a result, it can be surmised that there is a greater potential to achieve the maximization of the market value of the capital assets of the firm.

However, note that even an honest management does not have the necessary motivation to be efficient. For, while they are accountable for the costs and losses associated with their decisions, they do not receive returns which are commensurate with their efforts since they hold much less than 100 percent of the common stock of the company. See, for instance, Jensen and Meckling (1976, p.313), Watts and Zimmerman (1983), and Harris and Raviv (1991). This, in its turn, creates a possibility of opportunistic behavior (pursuit of self interest with guile) on the part of the management which can be at variance with the value maximization goals of the shareholders.

In sum, though the implicit contractual agreements result in information advantages the management may exhibit a high degree of moral hazard which is difficult to control.

See, for instance, Hoskisson and Turk (1990), and Jensen (1993).

Hence, as Jensen and Ruback (1983, p.43) put it, it is necessary for the board of directors to

(a) devise incentives and monitoring mechanisms which (i) attempt to align managerial objectives with their own, and (ii) require the management to bear the risks (through managerial shareholding) to ensure bonding, and

(b) place constraints on the managerial decision making to ensure compliance.

However, it was pointed out that these arrangements may be

(a) inadequate to ensure bonding, and/or

(b) more expensive to implement in comparison to the expected capital gains.

It is somewhat suprising that it has been much more difficult to obtain useful empirical information about the efficiency of the implicit contracts.

In the final analysis it appears that some amount of adverse selection and/or moral hazard[6] will persist in both types of control structures. As such the shareholders will be compelled to accept some reduction in the market value of the firm to ensure that the implicit contract or the governance mechanism is sustainable at an efficient level albeit a second best. See, for instance, Hill and Jones (1992, pp.134ff).

The following conclusions emerge from the analysis of this section.

(a) There are three alternative control mechanisms in the context of corporate control. There are certain advantages and shortcomings associated with each of the control systems.

(b) As Jensen and Warner (1988, p.3) remarked, "understanding the behavior of the corporate organization requires deeper knowledge of its governance and the factors that determine the distribution of power among the corporate managers, shareholders, and directors." For, as of now, the available evidences are at best fragmentary.

(c) A direct test of the prevalance of one of these organizational structures over the other would necessitate (i) estimating the several cost components associated with each of these decisions, and (ii) their relative valuation by the shareholders and the management.

However, as Harris and Raviv (1992, p.67), and Smith and Watts (1992, p.281) noted, this has not been possible so far for a variety of reasons. The details of this theme will be pursued in the sequel.

1.3 Managerial Discretion

Almost every firm in the oligopolistic market environment derives a positive profit from its operations at least in the short run. They also generate non-price strategies to maintain or augment these profits dynamically. This is usually one of the necessary conditions for the discretionary use of resources by the management. See, for instance, Gordon (1961, p.xii).

Even the owner manager of the neoclassical firm can be expected to pursue certain dynamic objectives. For, in oligopolistic markets, maintaining the market share to stay ahead of competition would have necessitated foregoing some of the profits. Two different aspects of such discretion have been identified.

(a) The firm will not pursue profit or the market value

maximization if it is in conflict with the attainment of other desirable objectives from a dynamic perspective. For all practical purposes the pursuit of other objectives increases the cost of production of the firm.

(b) The firm may generate maximum possible profits but it may be compelled to pay the workers and the lenders a part of these funds to ensure long run survival. In this framework discretion manifests itself at the level of the distribution of net gains.

Baumol's (1959) sales maximization hypothesis, Williamson's (1964) expense preference argument, and Marris's (1964) growth of capital assets formulation belong to the first category. In these theories the owner manager of the firm is postulated to divert resources away from profit or value maximization to achieve personal goals like the stability of the market share, security, and prestige. Also see, Lintner (1971, p. 218), and Yarrow (1976, p. 267). The organizational slack conceptualization of Cyert and March (1963), though it has some aspects in common with the first approach, belongs to the second category. For, they contend that the members of the production team, who have the most accurate information regarding the economic profits earned by the firm, will try to extract a part of these gains and the owner manager has to accept the organizational slack to keep the firm stable.

This argument suggests that even the board of directors, operating the firm under a governance mechanism, exercise such discretion.

In a modern corporation the seperation of ownership from control and the decentralization of the decision making powers result in two other aspects which give rise to managerial discretion, viz.,

(a) information asymmetry and adverse selection, and

(b) moral hazard.

The information asymmetry which the shareholders experience gives rise to the possibility that the managers of the firm can exercise authority and pursue personal goals in preference to corporate objectives. See, for instance, Kaysen (1959), Gordon (1961), and Jensen and Meckling (1976). Such managerial discretion can be expected to generate utility to the management in excess of the cost imposed on the shareholders.

The Marris (1964) hypothesis was originally formulated in the context of managerial decision making in decentralized organizations. In addition, Leibenstein (1980) argued that even while producing a given level of output and/or targetting a fixed growth of capital assets the management of the firm may prefer to reduce their effort thereby reducing productivity and inflating costs. Hoenack (1983) labels these as on the job leisure and resource diversions. Such managerial discretion results in increased costs. On the other hand, organizational slack can occur in the context of decentralized organizations as well. For, the divisional level demand to share profits generated by the firm cannot be ruled out.

To reduce these effects the board of directors makes an attempt to

(a) devise incentive mechanisms which align managerial objectives with their own (i.e., achieve bonding), and

(b) place some constraints on the managerial decision making to ensure compliance.

Stock options, bonus payments, and perquisites belong to the first group. The constraints may take the form of monitoring by auditing performance, or placing limits on the dividends per share. Both these approaches involve additional costs to the firm. As a result, the phenomenon of managerial discretion tends to perpetuate itself because as Jensen and Meckling (1976) put it, further incentive alignment would impose excessive risk bearing, monitoring and bonding costs. There are two pertinent points from the viewpoint of the rest of the study.

(a) There are many alternative specifications of the multiple goals of the management and discretionary managerial behavior. The theoretical arguments have not been sufficient to provide guidelines for a specific choice in a given empirical context. Yarrow (1973, and 1976, p. 267) stated the fundamental problem. As he put it, "once managerial discretion is allowed, economic theory can have little to say about the components and shapes of managerial utility functions." In particular, as Lintner (1971, p.218) suggested, it has not been possible to conceptualize "the relative weights to be given to 'equity value increasing' objectives and other elements in the utility functions of business as they affect and determine actual decision situations." Yarrow (1976, p.267) suggested that the "best that can be done is to hypothesize a particular type of objective function, explore its consequences, and where possible, test (the consequences of) the model against the evidence."

(b) From the empirical perspective, as Lintner (1971, p.218) remarked, the knowledge regarding managerial preferences remained incomplete since it has not been possible to estimate the relative weights which the management assigns to value increasing objectives and other aspects which they take into account. More recently, Schmalensee (1989, p. 957) acknowledged that the "data on endogenous variables (i.e., the actual choices of the management) do provide information, though not the sort that can be handled by the commonly employed estimation techniques." Radice (1971, p.549), and Cubbin and Leech (1986, p.124) recognized the existence of an identification problem that must be resolved. There has been a very limited progress on the empirical front as a result of these fundamental conceptual difficulties.

Further details of both these aspects will be taken up at an appropriate place in the sequel.

This section can be concluded by noting that there have been difficulties in identifying the

(a) ex ante sources of managerial discretion, and
(b) patterns of behavior implicit in the ex post or observed manifestations of such discretion.

The analysis of corporate control in a modern corporation will remain incomplete until progress can be made in

(a) developing organizational economics concepts to explain the behavior within the firms as Barney (1986, p.141), and Kay (1991, p.62) pointed out, and
(b) constructing empirical procedures to infer the patterns of managerial discretion from the observed performance of the firms.

1.4 An Outline of the Present Study

With these arguments in perspective the present study attempts to examine the following three aspects of the problem:

(a) As a first step an attempt will be made to identify (i) the locus of control – the governance mechanism or the implicit contract - of any given firm[7], and (ii) the reasons for the specific choice.

(b) A modelling exercise will be developed to determine the direction and extent of managerial discretion in the context of a specific firm. Three aspects need attention in this endeavor: (i) the two major theoretical contributions concerning the corporate control and capital structure decisions, viz., the Marris (1964) model and the bonding hypothesis of Grossman and Hart (1982) should be kept in perspective, (ii) the models should also describe the channels through which incentives and constraints modify managerial behavior and quantify the extent of success achieved by these instruments in relation to the shareholders' quest to realign objectives, and (iii) since the necessity for a resolution of the identification problem has been recorded a simple estimation method, based on the fundamental economic reasoning underlying the decision making process, will have to be developed.

(c) Detailed empirical estimates for several firms in the chemical industry will be developed to provide insights into the managerial decision making process at work.

In sum, this study is a first step, albeit an important one, to make fundamental progress in the area of corporate control and strategic financial decisions of modern corporations.

However, to keep the theoretical as well as the empirical work within manageable limits it will be assumed that the short term operating decisions with respect to the utilization of capital assets are invariabily delegated to the management, and efficiently chosen by the management.

The rest of the study is organized as follows: Chapter 2 reviews the pertinent literature on corporate control and identifies the essential aspects which should receive attention in the modelling effort. A recursive model will be specified to make the distinction between the operation of the different control mechanisms in chapter 3. The method of identifying the reasons for any one specific choice will also be outlined. Chapter 4 sets up the model of managerial discretion in the context of the capital structure choice. A method of estimation and several operational details in its implementation will also be specified. The details of the data and the definitions of the variables used in the study will be detailed in chapter 5. Chapter 6 examines the empirical result of the model of the organizational mechanism. The results of the managerial discretion exercise will be theme of chapter 7. Chapter 8 provides a retrospect on the basic achievements of the study, a summary of some of the limitations which need further attention, and statement on future directions of research.

The history of the firms, which was used as a supplement while interpreting the empirical results, is offered as an appendix to facilitate the reader's appraisal of the analysis.

On the whole, this study is a basic contribution to the area of corporate control and the capital structure decision. Significant empirical work, which eluded the analysts for so long, can now be developed along these lines in the near future.

NOTES

1. Turnovsky (1970, p.1064) defines the business risk as the variability in the earnings of the firm resulting from the uncertainty in the demand for the products of the firm. This will be distinct from the financial risk associated with a specific choice of capital structure. For, the capital assets of the firm can be financed by both debt and equity. Hence, the fixed interest obligation of debt financing as a proportion of net sales defines the financial risk.
2. In an environment where the business risks are high the need for frequent adjustments in the decisions makes the task even more difficult.

3. The governance structure usually consists of (a) laws governing corporate behavior and its attendent legal apparatus, and (b) monitoring mechanisms (like the board of directors), and enforcement mechanisms (such as the market for corporate control and managerial labor market). See, for instance, Hill and Jones (1992, p.67.).
4. Two different aspects of this argument should be noted. (a) Due to the information asymmetry and the transaction costs which the shareholders experience the market price of common stock may be inadequate to ensure an efficient performance of firms. (b) If other organizational arrangements eventually supplement the capital market it is still possible that (i) information asymmetry persists, (ii) there can be adverse selection in the process of choosing the directors or the managers, and (iii) moral hazard is a possible manifestation. The capital market cannot ensure efficient contractual performance due to these frictions.
5. The internal capital market notion is popular in the M-Form literature. However, note that the organization of the firm along M-Form lines is not necessary for the existence of an internal capital market. Further, much of the M-Form literature deals with the allocation of a given amount of physical and financial capital among the different product divisions of the firm. The capital structure decision rarely receives the attention it deserves. Williamson (1988) emphasizes only the asset specificity of the physical assets in the choice of the debt equity ratio. The crucial dimension of information and control are missing from the analysis.
6. Adverse selection has been defined in the following manner. Suppose one of the parties in a contract experience information asymmetry. The better informed party can utilize this to influence the terms of the contract in its favour. However, opportunism is not restricted to the precontractual stage. For, suppose the behavior of at least one party to a contract is unobservable ex post. However, such behavior can have an influence on the payoffs to both parties. In such cases there is always a potential for the party who has the information advantage to modify its behavior to the detriment of the welfare of the other. That is, the classic moral hazard problem exists ex post.
7. Given any control mechanism, the decisions of the management and the resulting corporate performance will have an effect on the share price of the firm if the secondary markets are active

[liquid, as Grossman and Miller (1988), and Holstrom and Tirole (1993) put it.]. However, it cannot be taken for granted that the changes in the share prices will induce the management to alter their decisions. Hence, to the extent that the market for corporate control is inefficient it can only provide a broad framework within which the other control systems function. It does not have the role of an independent control mechanism.

2

Corporate Control: Theory and Evidence

2.1 An Overview

As stated in section 1.4 the two basic objectives of this study are the following.

(a) To identify the locus of control, i.e.,
   (i) the nature of control, and
   (ii) the reasons for the specific choices of any given firm.

(b) An analysis of the dimensions of the discretionary use of resources and their quantitative impact on the market value of the firm.

Consequently, the review of the literature is organized in the following manner.

(a) A significant part of the studies on corporate control considers the nature of the ownership of the firm as the basic determinant of the voting rights and corporate control. In other words, it is generally postulated that ownership provides an ex ante measure of corporate control and the locus of control can be inferred without any reference to the decision making behavior. Despite the attractive conceptual basis this approach has its limitations. Section 2.2 reviews the literature which considers various ex ante measures of corporate control.

(b) The alternative is to argue that the board of directors or the management, having gained control, makes the strategic decisions according to their own preferences. Hence, an analysis of the pattern of the ex post choices of the firm can reveal the locus of control. This approach necessitates (i) a specification of the most important strategic decisions which can provide an accurate inference about the locus of control, (ii) an identification of the constraints and objectives in the decision making process, and (iii) a specification of the method through which the inference will be drawn. The advantage of this procedure is that the dimensions of managerial discretion can be estimated along with the inference regarding the locus of control. However, the information requirements for obtaining an efficient inference is its major drawback.

It can be concluded that the survey would reveal the specific advantages and shortcomings of both the approaches and provide specific guidelines for improving the analysis. Hence, section 2.3

(a) examines the nature of strategic decisions that require exploration,

(b) identifies the specific models utilized, and

(c) the inference procedures in studies which use the ex post approach to the identification of the locus of corporate control.

Section 2.4 will summarize the tasks for the present study with this experience in perspective.

2.2 The Ex ante Approach

This approach considers the following aspects while determining the locus of control:

(a) Stockownership and voting rights,
(b) Managerial shareholding,
(c) Composition of the board of directors,
(d) Capital structure as reflected in the debt equity ratio,
(e) Asset specificity,
(f) The urgency of making decisions in a competitive product market, and
(g) The risks and losses involved in the markets and specific decisions of the firm.

Many of these factors may be such that they indicate the necessity for a closer monitoring and control of managerial decisions in an implicit contract rather than its replacement by a comprehensive governance procedure. With this in perspective each of these aspects may now be considered in detail. However, it should be kept in mind that providing a specific and exhaustive set of references from the vast literature is a very difficult task.

Stock ownership and voting rights have been often considered as the factors which determine the ability of the shareholders, or the board of directors as their representatives, to exercise control and/or offer a potential threat to exercise control. Two measures are generally adopted: (i) the extent of shareholding by one person or a cohesive group[1], and (ii) the percentage of legally determined voting rights vested in a specific group which can block a strategic decision at a meeting of the shareholders. Nyman and Silberston (1978) labeled these as the behavioral and structural procedures. There are three difficulties with this approach: (i) there cannot be any objective specification of the limits of the threshold where the control changes hands, (ii) event studies about the actual change of control may not provide sufficient generalization, and (iii) these shareholding limits may not be effective in enforcing control due to the inefficiency of the stock market even when there is a takeover threat.

The percentage of shareholding which provides corporate control[2] varies from one industry to another and across countries. Jacquemin and DeJong (1977, p.165), and Carney (1987) noted that 25 percent shareholding provides control in the context of Germany. Berle and Means (1932), Palmer (1973), Bothwell (1990), and Leech and Leahy (1991) proposed very different estimates. However, it is possible to argue that control can be gained in some situations well before any such threshold is reached. For, instance, Larner (1966, p.779, footnote 5) quoted an example where 3.9 percent shareholding by a family provided control of the firm.

The inadequacy of these measures to provide effective corporate control can be explained as follows. Suppose for the sake of the argument that a common threshold limit can be specified. If the company is not doing well and there is a takeover threat this group of the shareholders may not sell their holding because they expect to maintain control as well as obtain the capital gains even if the takeover is effected. However, the possibility of the emergence of a new controlling coalition cannot be ruled out.

On the whole, this analysis based on the event studies could not provide an adequate generalization though they provide useful information in specific contexts.

The shareholders offer stock ownership to the management in their effort to ensure bonding[3]. For, if they have to make and enforce efficient decisions under asymmetric information the costs of monitoring and bonding will be too high. See, for instance, Oliner and Rudebusch (1992, p.644). However, when the managerial ownership of the common stock is low their share of dividends is too small for them to bond with the shareholders in their quest for value maximization. That is, only a high enough shareholding will induce them to bond with the shareholders. This argument was advanced in Flath and Knoeber (1985), Jarrell and Poulsen (1988), and Jensen and Warner (1988). However, a high percentage of shareholding enables the management to gain corporate control. In an empirical context Schliefer and Vishny (1986), and Morck, Schliefer and Vishny (1988) found that the management gains control whenever their shareholding is between 5 and 25 percent of the common stock. However, the consensus appears to suggest that the management gains control whenever they hold 10 percent or more of the common stock. See, for instance, Larner (1966), Jacquemin and DeJong (1977), and Chang and Choi (1988).

All members of the board of directors are charged, by statute, with the task of protecting the interest of the shareholders. In general, the board of directors will have some inside directors representing the management and some outside directors appointed by the shareholders. The primary role of the inside directors is decision management while that of the outside directors is decision control. See, for instance, Fama and Jensen (1983), and Rediker and Seth (1995). Fama and Jensen (1983), in particular, hypothesize that outside directors have the reputation as experts in controlling the decisions of the firms in such a way as to align them with the objectives of the shareholders. Also see, Brickley and James (1987). The composition of the board of directors, in terms of the relative proportion of the inside and outside directors, varies considerably from one firm to another. A comparative study for the U.S.A. and the U.K. by Cosh and Hughes (1987) indicates that the non-executive directors constitute 37 percent of the average of the U.K. boards compared to 65 percent for the U.S.A. boards. However, it is difficult to draw any inference regarding the locus of control from these figures. In the context of Germany and Japan the banks have a major role in financing industry. Their representatives on the board of directors exercise control. See, for instance, Cable (1988), and Aoki (1990).

However, the executive directors may not exercise the requisite control for several reasons. (i) They may not have any significant financial interest since the payments they receive are not proportional to the profits or the market value. (ii) They may be busy people (often they hold positions in many firms) and have little time to think about the company's affairs or to collect information. (iii) The non-executive (outside) directors may owe their position to the managers so that they can be reelected and continue to collect their fees. See, for instance, Hart (1995), and Thompson (1988).

Jensen (1993) argued that when the strength of the board exceeds seven or eight individuals they are less likely to function effectively and the CEO (Chief executive officer) gains control. For, generally the CEO holds the position of the chairman of the board of directors. In the U.K. the Cadbury Committee recommended that it is necessary to keep the roles of the chairman and the CEO seperate if the shareholders wish to retain an effective control.

The debt equity ratio[4] has often been utilized as an alternative measure to reflect the extent of managerial control on corporate decisions. Grossman and Hart (1982, pp.108ff) argued that the potential profit that can be generated is high if the debt equity ratio is low. The managers may then gain control, incur some agency costs, and divert resources to satisfy their personal interest. On the other hand, if the debt equity ratio is high, the profit potential would be low but the management would be under great pressure to generate it. This approach suggests that a low debt equity ratio provides greater control to the management. However, as Stultz (1988), and Harris and Raviv (1988) pointed out, a high debt equity ratio reduces the strength of outside control and provides the management with far greater control rights.

In general, this approach could not clearly define the nature and extent of managerial control which a given capital structure choice entails.

Williamson (1988) argued that equity financing, which

affords more intrusive monitoring and involvement through the board of directors, is the preferred financial instrument for projects where there is significant asset specificity.For, suppose the resale or liquidation value of such specific assets is low. The shareholders are likely to lose substantially if the management is not efficient. The shareholders will consider it more prudent to exercise greater control over the strategic decisions. Also see, Watts and Zimmerman (1983), Fama (1990, p.S77), and Ofek (1993, p.5). The following counter argument is also recorded in the literature. Suppose the capital assets of the firm are highly specific to its production lines and the shareholders do not have the expertise to make efficient decisions. For the efficient functioning of such a firm an implicit contract becomes inevitable because the shareholders must delegate the decision making responsibilities to the managers.

Managerial control in a decentralized organization has the advantage of reducing the cost of decision making but these advantages are accompanied by coordination problems which lead to delay and/or duplication of effort. Consequently decentralization is desirable when there is little urgency or a great deal of private information. But it is inefficient if there is an urgency to make decisions or the management does not have adequate information. See, for instance, Bolton and Farrell (1990). The effective locus of control may be determined by these considerations.

Leech and Leahy (1991) argued that when there is a high degree of business risk, frequent adjustments are required in the deployment of productive assets. The shareholders and the board of directors do not have an advantage in such cases. Control will be generally delegated to the management. However, following Wiliiamson (1964), Monsen and Downs (1965), and Baumol (1967) it can be argued that the executives of manager controlled firms are likely to exhibit risk averse behavior due to the asymmetries in the managers' reward structure and the increase in the market value of the firm. It would then be necessary for the shareholders to regain control. See, for instance, Stultz (1990).

On the whole, it is evident that each of these aspects is important in determining the locus of control. However, the ex ante approach has been subject to two limitations:

(a) the ex ante measures cannot satisfactorily explain the reasons why the management can be deemed to have gained control when these variables attain certain threshold values, and
(b) the numerical limits on each of these variables, which may bring the corporation under the control of the management, largely depend on the industrial setting and the environment external to the firm so that any generalization is hazardous.

The alternative is to pursue an ex post approach.

2.3 The Ex post Approach

For purpose of clarity of exposition it would be convenient to divide this section into three parts:

(a) long term decisions,
(b) the variables which influence the decisions, and
(c) the inference procedures.

A review of the literature on each of three aspects will be taken up sequentially.

2.3.1 Long Term Decisions

The corporate strategy of the firms is invariably directed towards well defined objectives like the market value and market share. The firm generally tries to utilize its distinctive competencies[5] to convert the market prospects to profits and market value. Two decisions are of paramount importance in this context:

(a) the growth of capital assets of the firm, and
(b) the capital structure decision represented by the debt equity ratio.

This aspect of the decision making process can be detailed in the following manner.

One theory emerging from the literature on monopolistic competition, argues that

(a) there are generally limits on the demand for the primary products of the firm leading to excess capacity,
(b) economies of scale in production cannot be fully exploited if the firm restricts itself to a single product,
(c) in its quest for larger profits the firm may diversify into related products, and
(d) the existence of market potential leads to such diversification even if there are no economies of scope.

More pertinently, the introduction of new products may require (especially in the latter case) certain additional investments in plant and machinery. This process initiates the growth of the capital assets of the firm.

The second theory has its origin in the managerial response to business risk. Assume that either

(a) due to reasons extraneous to the functioning of the firm or the industry of which it is a part, or
(b) due to the actions and reactions of rival firms in the market (including potential entry),

the demand curve for the primary product of the firm is random. Lintner (1971, pp.172 ff) contains an early statement of this position. Also see, Hassid (1977). To reduce such uncertainties the firm may resort to product diversification. Once again, depending upon the nature of the diversification strategy, there will be a necessity for the growth of the fixed assets of the firm[6].

The third theory emphasizes dimensions of non-price competition which affect the demand curve for the products of the firm[7]. For, as Marris (1971a, p.10, and 1971b, p.270) put it succintly, search, research, development, and selling expenditures can have the effect of stabilizing and/or shifting the demand curves to the right. In other words, as Fillipi and Zanetti (1971, p.147) argued, the firm may attempt a growth process at the expense of competitors.

Fillipi and Zanetti (1971, p.150) also argued that an increase in the labor costs and trade union problems may induce substitution of capital for labor given the volume of output. This acts as a stimulus for new investments, greater productivity of capital and growth of the capital assets of the firm.

From the current perspective it is important to realize that all these theories are valid irrespective of the locus of corporate control.

The contrast is provided by theories which emphasize the seperation of ownership from control. When the management gains control they may be

(a) inclined, on their own volition, to pursue growth, or

(b) induced by the shareholders, who provide appropriate incentives to achieve the growth rate that they desire[8].

The management may value the growth decision for the following reasons:

(a) as Francis (1980, p.355) pointed out it enables the firm to convert market prospects to profits,

(b) as noted in Fillipi and Zanetti (1971, p.147) it can stimulate growth in the productivity of labor and reduce labor union problems,

(c) as Marris (1964, p.102 and 106) observed successful expansion of assets enables the management to recommend itself to the more lucrative jobs that it creates, and

(d) increased size becomes a deterrent to takeover raids and enhances the job security of the managers. See, for instance, Kamecke (1993).

Hence, as Marris (1964, pp.46ff) summed it up, growth of capital assets of the firm provides the management power, prestige, and job security.

As a result, growth becomes a motive for not only collective but individual enhancement. In essence, it is possible that the management controlled firms will exhibit faster rates of growth.

These plans for the growth of assets will be conditioned by the availability of finances. See, for instance, Vickers (1968, and 1987), Lintner (1971), and Fillipi and Zanetti (1971). In particular, for a given choice of the rate of growth of capital assets the firm has the choice of an optimal debt equity ratio. Several studies indicate that the specific choice of the debt equity ratio is related to

(a) profitability [Donaldson (1961), and Brealey and Myers (1984)],

(b) growth of the capital assets [Jensen and Meckling (1976), Smith and Warner (1979), and Green (1984)],

(c) non-debt tax shields [DeAngelo and Masulis (1980)], and

(d) asset structure [Myers and Majluf (1984), and Williamson(1988)].

Since the emphasis of the present study is on the control dimension, the bonding property of the debt equity ratio pointed out by Grossman and Hart (1982) will be highlighted.

Grossman and Hart (1982, p.109) noted that management chooses the debt equity ratio in such a way as to bring their own objectives "into line with those of the shareholders because of the effect on market value. In other words the management bonds itself to act in the shareholders' interest." Jensen (1986, p.324) popularised the idea that "debt creation enables the managers to effectively bond their promise to payoff future cashflows." Blazenko (1987), Thompson (1988), and Harris and Raviv (1990), Stultz (1990), and Hart (1995) formalized a similar argument.

On the other hand, the emergence of managerial discretion cannot be ruled out. For, as Stultz (1988), and Harris and Raviv (1988) argued, a high debt equity ratio reduces the control of the outside directors and provides the management with far greater control rights.

For all practical purpose, the growth of capital assets, and the capital structure can be regarded as the major strategic decisions of the firm.

However, there is as yet no objective criterion to decide which, among a given set of variables, is a relevant decision. The following argument is illustrative.

(a) Suppose there is a business risk implicit in the product market conditions. Clearly, this can be expected to have an effect on the market value of the firm. However, it may not be possible for the decision makers within the firm to influence it. In general, such variables will be included in the specifications as exogenous influences on the market value and not as decision variables.

(b) Consider a variable like the managerial shareholding. Is this a relevant decision variable? Assume that the governance mechanism is in operation. The board of directors will choose this to ensure that their decisions regarding growth and capital structure are properly implemented. This decision does not have an independent effect on the potential maximum of the market value of the firm. It will not be considered as an independent long term decision. Suppose, on the other hand, that the control mechanism is an implicit contract. Even in this case it is a decision of the board of directors. The management is expected to choose the growth and capital structure on the basis of this incentive constraint. Hence, it cannot have an independent effect on the market value of the firm. In general, the strategic variables chosen for analysis must have independent effects.

(c) However, more recent research has been highlighting the interactive effects of long term decisions. See, for instance, Rao and Saha (1994), Radiker and seth (1995) and the reference cited therein. It is necessary to take this aspect into account in the modelling exercise.

On the whole, there is a scope for judgement of the analyst in the choice of the decision variables. At least on some occasions it would be posssible to say that certain decisions which are excluded from the analysis are far more important compared to those that are included. There is no satisfactory approach to guard against this danger.

2.3.2 *The Variables which Influence the Decisions*

A fairly thorough search through the literature indicated that the decision models have not been structured systematically while examining the factors which influence the long term decisions. Instead partial sets of hypotheses regarding each of the decisions have been proposed.

An attempt will be made in this section to present these results within the framework of a systematic model. Consider the governance mechanism. It is to be expected that

$$v = v(g, \theta, x)$$

where v = potential market value of the firm

g = rate of growth of capital assets

θ = debt equity ratio, and

x = a vector of variables which enter the shareholders' assesment of the market value of the firm.

In general, x will include three types of variables:

(a) the market conditions external to the firm,

(b) the distinctive competencies of the firm, and

(c) the organizational mechanisms which translate the potential to competitive advantage.

See, for example, Kay (1995).

Consider the values of g and θ which maximize v. They can be represented by

$$g = g(x)$$

$$\theta = \theta(x)$$

The board of directors would like to entice the management to execute these decisions. However, they recognize that the actual choice will depend on the incentives y offered to the management[9]. That is, the realized choices will satisfy the equations

$$g_a = g_a(x, y), \text{ and}$$

$$\theta_a = \theta_a(x, y)$$

Consequently, the board can be expected to choose y in such a way

$$g_a = g(x), \text{ and}$$

$$\theta_a = \theta(x)$$

That is, in general,

$$y = y(x)$$

If the implicit contract is in operation the management will choose g and θ so as to

$$\text{Maximize } u = u(v, g, \theta, y)$$

$$\text{subject to } v = v(g, \theta, x)$$

$$\text{where } u = \text{managerial preferences.}$$

Hence, in general, it is expected that

$$g = g(x, y), \text{ and}$$

$$\theta = \theta(x, y)$$

However, the board of directors cannot have the information about the functions $g(x, y)$, and $\theta(x, y)$. Instead, they observe the g and the θ decisions of the management. Consequently they will choose y to maximize v so that

$$y = y(g, \theta, x)$$

It is however obvious that these specifications leave considerable scope

(a) for specifying the hierarchy of decisions,

(b) regarding the use of incentive constraints in the decision making,

(c) about the extent to which reduced forms can be used for inference.

Both these formulations have one thing in common. They specify the g, θ, and y equations in detail and utilize them to develop the desired inference. Since the literature is fairly extensive it will reviewed so that the appropriate information can be utilized in the rest of the study.

Referring to section 2.3.1 once again it should be noted that the major determinants of the growth of capital assets are the business risk, distinctive competencies represented by the specificity of the asset structure and organizational design, financial risk implicit in the choice of the capital structure and ownership rights and the incentives provided to the management. Most of the studies, including Marris (1964), and Cubbin and Leech (1986) acknowledged this.

As Harris and Raviv (1992, p.67) remarked, the major determinants of the capital structure decision in different environments are not clearly understood. Only two aspects are generally highlighted. They are the business risk, and the availability and cost of specific financial instruments (generally designated as the financial risk). These will be examined sequentially.

It is generally expected that an increase in the business risk would induce the firm to finance a greater proportion of its capital assets through the capital market. The primary justification for this is the necessity to spread risks under limited liability. On the other hand, the firm may resort to debt financing for the following reasons:

(a) Grossman and Hart (1982) argued that the management may issue some debt to convince the shareholders that they will align their goals with them.

(b) Fama (1990, p.S89) pointed out that the managers may consider the issue of bonds as a way to convince the shareholders of their bonding by providing centralized monitoring of default risks by financial intermediaries, auditors and so on who specialize in evaluating such risks.[10]

(c) In some cases, the current cashflows and internal source of finance may be inadequate to take the advantage of the emerging market prospects. In such cases the firm resorts to debt financing. However, as Vickers (1987, pp.28 ff) argued, there will be an increase in the interest rates on debt financing as the debt equity ratio increases. Hence, the expected profitability of the proposed investment puts a limit on the debt equity ratio.

(d) The firms which experience high transaction costs in the capital market prefer to issue debt to finance their capital assets. See, for instance, Taub (1975), and Titman and Wessels (1988).

Three other aspects are considered in the choice of the debt equity ratio.

(a) In general, the more specific the assets the less will be their liquidation value and the consequent risk in cases where the firm experiences any business risk at all. The more risky specific assets will then be financed by equity and the less specific assets by debt[11]. See, for instance, Williamson (1988), and Smith and Watts (1992).

(b) Whenever a firm experiences short term liquidity problems in a fluctuating product market they would need to utilize a part of the reserves and surpluses to conduct current transactions. This limits the availability of funds for investments. As a result the debt equity ratio will be affected. The most recent reiteration of this argument is in Fazzari and Peterson (1993).

(c) It would appear, on apriori grounds, that the managerial decisions regarding the growth of capital assets would have a bearing on the management's choice of the debt equity ratio. Smith and Watts (1992) argued that an increase in the rate of growth of capital assets cannot be financed by increasing the debt equity ratio due to the potential of bankruptcy if there is any business risk. On the other hand, Koutsoyiannis (1978) argued that an increase in the debt equity ratio may not pose any threats since an increase in the rate of growth of assets is a satisfactory indicator of the future prospects of the firm .

Turning to the *y* variables the literature emphasizes

(a) Wages and other compensation[12] as the major incentive, and

(b) dividend payment requirement as the major constraint in the context of the decision making process.

Consider the factors which influence the choice of wage payments. In some of the earlier literature, like McGuire et al (1962), it was pointed out that the wage payments are mostly related to the past performance and that they cannot be interpreted as having any incentive effects. However, most of the recent studies acknowledge that the wage payments vary with the strategies of the firm and environmental considerations. Three major arguments are discernible:

(a) Most of them conclude that wage payments are a function of size indicated by the level of sales. See, for instance, Flath and Knoeber (1985), Coughlan and Schmidt (1985), Mueller (1986, pp.158ff), Skilvas (1987), and Garvey and Gaston (1991)[13]. Viewed as an incentive to the management wages and salaries tend to increase with size "because the costs of incorrect decisions are vastly greater in large firms than in small ones."- Conyon and Leech (1994, p.232).

(b) Since wage payments are an incentive it can be argued that a part of the profits will be paid to the workers and the managers. Studies of Mueller (1986, ch.7), and Conyon and Leech (1994) represent a small sample. On occasions it was pointed out that wage payments may be related to the performance of stock prices. This may happen if the long term component or the fixity of wages is predominant. For, changes in share prices will then reflect the changes in the market value of the firm. See, for instance, Conyon, Gregg, and Machin (1995).

(c) In some studies it was pointed out that when the proportion of outside members on the board of directors is large the management needs to be given wage incentives to ensure efficient performance. A few recent studies in this direction are Mehran (1995), and Hambrick and Finkelstein (1995).

However, it should be noted that the identification of efficient incentives in incomplete contracts is as yet controversial. See, for instance, Milgrom and Roberts (1992, chs.12 and 13).

Studies related to dividend decisions are rather extensive. This literature considers the distinction between the shareholder versus management decision to be fundamental. In the early literature Lintner (1956) argued that the shareholders prefer to claim a steady rate of dividend whenever there is a significant business risk in order to avoid the prospect of not being able to recover adequate returns through long run capital gains. On the other hand, it was pointed out that the growth oriented management would need to keep the shareholders satisfied while building a steady base of reserves and surpluses for investment purposes. As Grabowsky and Mueller (1972, p.10) put it, "some dividends will probably be paid because they yield utility to the managers by increasing their security against a takeover." Despite such clarity sought out in some studies the bulk of the literature failed to keep the two approaches distinct.

Consider, an increase in the business risk. A DeAlessi and Fishe (1987), and Kort (1990, p.377) pointed out, we may expect the possibility of opportunistic behavior by managers who increase the investment in the firm. This increases the risk of the firm going bankrupt before the dividend payment starts. The shareholders claim higher dividends as soon as possible to avoid such a contingency. Also refer to Jorgensen et al (1989, pp.339 and 365).

The above argument also implies that if the management were to decide the dividends they will reduce it as the business risk increases. Rozeff (1982, p.251) stated this very clearly. Consider two firms with the same average cashflows but different business risk. The firm which experiences a greater business risk will need to finance externally in bad years. In addition to the constraints on external finances it will also experience higher cost of financing[14]. Consequently, the management chooses a lower dividend payout ratio.

However, as Copeland and Weston (1988, p.564) succintly put it, this may not happen. For, the managers may have to signal to the shareholders that they expect sufficiently large future cashflows to fulfil their debt and dividend obligations[15]. Grabowski and Mueller (1972, p.21) have gone to the extent of arguing that the management will increase dividend payments with an increase in the business risk[16]. It is therefore not surprising to find Copeland and Weston (1988, p.554) pointing out that dividend decisions may be independent of business risk. For, an increase in the dividend payment today will result in an equivalent reduction in the ex dividend price of the common stock in the future. The market value of the firm remains invariant.

Business risk increases with asset specificity. Smith and

Watts (1992, p.274) reported that the shareholders take out greater dividends in such a context.

As remarked in Walter (1963, p.287), Rozeff (1982, p.251), and succintly summarized in Copeland and Weston (1988, p.568), management, when they are making the dividend decision may consider it as a bonding device. For, given the extent of investment which they undertake, an increase in dividends requires a greater reliance on external financing and greater scrutiny of their decisions.

Consider the effect of the shareholding by the managers and their relatives. One standard argument is that the managers, as part owners of the firm would automatically bond better and that the need to utilize dividends as a bonding signal has diminished. See, for instance, Rozeff (1982 p.250). But the opposite argument is equally pervasive. For, now that the managers are experiencing the nondiversifiable business risk they would prefer to increase their incomes by paying out more.

What effect would other managerial decisions have on the choice of dividend decisions? Consider the managerial choice of growth of capital assets. In general as Walter (1963, p.280), and Vickers (1968, and 1987) argued, the net cashflows constrain the investment and dividend choices[17]. For, they are available for

(a) the payment of interest and repayment of debts,

(b) financing capital expenditures, and

(c) dividend payments

As a result, the increase in the costs of financing the growth of fixed assets by external sources induces the management to reduce the dividend payments. The effect of the capital structure on dividends operates essentially through bondholder perceptions. Firstly, Easterbrook (1984, p.653) argued that as the debt equity ratio increases the bondholders want to limit dividends to prevent shareholders from opting for risky investment once the interest rate is set. Secondly, as Copeland and Weston (1988, pp.569-70) pointed out, an increase in the debt equity ratio would compel the shareholders to be more vigilant so that they are not subjected to loss by paying off greater dividends.

On the whole, it can be concluded that attempts to test such hypotheses utilized reduced form specifications. As Mueller (1967, pp.59-60) put it, "in writing each equation the researcher makes explicit assumptions only regarding the variables the entrepreneur considers relevant for each decision and not about the motives behind these decisions. One's perception regarding the goals of the firm are often introduced via the selection of the predetermined variables to be included in each equation." Even the best known study of Grabowski and Mueller (1972) can be classified only in this category. Such specifications do not capture the essential aspects of managerial discretion. Further, they are also valid even if the management pursues value maximization as the only objective. As a result they cannot offer any insight into the nature of managerial preference. See, for instance, Mueller (1986, p.164) and Schmalensee (1988, p.672).

2.4 The Empirical Results

Virtually all the empirical tests of the Marris (1964) model center around the adequacy of its predictions. In particular, after controlling for other influences, the question posed concerns the higher rates of growth of managerially controlled firms[18]. The results reported in Singh and Whittington (1968), Eatwell (1971), Marris (1971c), Radice (1971), Francis (1980), Cubbin and Leech (1986), and surveyed in detail in Nyman and Silberston (1978) generally negate the Marris hypothesis.

Two basic arguments have been put forward to explain these findings.

(a) Monsen and Downs (1965) argued that the risk

averse managers may attach greater disutility to failure and loss of job than they would to the power and prestige associated with success[19].

(b) Francis (1980) argued that growth of profits is the first priority of the managers and that the growth of assets which they will support will be strictly related to the attainment of this objective. Personal satisfaction, obtained from the growth of the firm, would rarely (if ever) get priority.

Consider the choice of the capital structure next. Turnovsky (1970), Taub (1975), Ferri and Jones (1979), and many others reported that an increase in the business risk tends to reduce the debt equity ratio. On the other hand, Marsh (1982) found the risk variables to be the least important in explaining the observed debt equity ratios. Kim and Sorensen (1986), and Rao, Rastogi, and Saha (1995) also reported that the negative sign materializes if the shareholders governance is the dominant form of corporate control.

The size of the firm, represented by the net capital assets of the firm, had a positive association in the empirical work of Taub (1975) and Titman and Wessels (1988). However, Smith and Watts (1992) found a negative relationship. Similarly, the studies of Koutsoyiannis (1978, and 1987) did not find the size variables to be significant in explaining the observed variations in the debt equity ratio.

The empirical work of Titman and Wessels (1988), and Balakrishnan and Fox (1993) reported only a peripheral support for the asset specificity hypothesis of Williamson (1988).

With respect to the effect of managerial shareholding on the choice of the capital structure Agrawal and Mandelker (1986), and Kim and Sorensen (1986) reported a positive association while Koutsoyiannis (1978), and Friend and Lang (1988) reported a negative relationship.

The empirical results of Kim and Sorensen (1986), and Smith and Watts (1992) indicate a reduction in the debt equity ratio as the growth rate of capital assets increases. Koutsoyiannis (1978) reported a positive association. However, Titman and Wessels (1988) did not find the rate of growth of capital assets to be significant in explaining the observed variations in the debt equity ratio.

Studies on wage payments and compensation schemes generally indicate a significant size effect. Similarly, firms with large outside board membership indicate a greater managerial compensation. Both of these suggest a risk aversion on the part of the shareholders. See, for instance, Mueller (1986), and Conyon and Leech (1994). However, neither profits nor the stock prices are significant. The results of Mueller (1986), Conyon and Leech (1994), and Conyon et al (1995) are, once again, representative. Ex ante committment in sharing risks is more important for risk reduction in such principal-agent formulations.

Even the empirical experiences with respect to dividend payments exhibit a mixed trend. Grabowski and Mueller (1972) reported a positive relationship between business risk and dividends. However, Rozeff (1982), and Koutsoyiannis (1987) found a negative association.

Rozeff (1982), as well as Rao, Rastogi, and Saha (1995) reported a negative relationship between managerial shareholding and dividends. The results of Smith and Watts (1992) are counter to it.

Most of the studies in the Indian context have tested the Lintner (1956) proposition and found it to be significant. See, for instance, Krishnamurty and Sastry (1975), Kisore (1981), Misra (1984), and Balasubrmaniam (1993). Only Rao and Sharma (1984), and Sharma (1986) made extensive efforts to distinguish between managerial and shareholder driven dividends decision. Two conclusions of Rao and Sharma (1984, pp.66 and 70) may be recalled:

(a) Though firms are attempting long run investment policies to increase the market value of the firm the shareholders are not convinced about the prospects of capital gains to a point where they would be willing to tradeoff dividend payments for capital gains. They would prefer to obtain a steady payment of dividends. The shareholders view the dividend decisions to be primary from a long run perspective.

(b) In cases where the management considered dividend decisions to be primary the constraints on external financing and the reliance on internal funds for investment made them feel that payingoff a steady stream of dividends will reduce shareholder antagonism.

On the whole, the empirical evidences are contradictory and fragmentary. No meaningful attempt has been made to resolve the differences of opinion.

2.5 Inferences about Managerial Preferences

Many unsuccessful attempts have been made to estimate such models. It can be shown that these attempts have been unsatisfactory due to an inappropriate

(a) choice of functional forms, and/or

(b) identification of the economic basis from which the requisite information can be extracted.

Most of the studies assume that the valuation frontier can be represented by

$$v = a_0 + a_1 g^2 + a_2 x$$

Similarly, the managerial preference function is written as

$$u = v + \lambda_1 g + \lambda_2 y$$

indicating a tradeoff between v and g. It follows that the value of g which maximizes u is given by

$$g^* = -(\lambda_1/2a_1)$$

This choice of g^* is independent of x and y. In general, this specification fails to explain the observed variation in g^*.

The first basic approach to the estimation problem started with the observation that the convexity of the preference function (indicating the manager's willingness to forgo a certain amount of v to achieve a higher g) would manifest itself in the form of a negative correlation between the observed values[20] of v and g as in Figure 2.1(a). Radice (1971) rejected the Marris model on the basis of an observed positive correlation between v and g. This inference is erroneous[21]. For, the above g^* equation does not provide a basis for the assumption that the locus of the observed (v, g) values would be negatively sloped if $\lambda_1 > 0$. For, as represented in Figure 2.1(b), it may have a positive slope. For the specific problem under consideration it indicates that the expansion path

$$v = a_0 - a_1 g^2 - \lambda_1 g + a_2 x.$$

would be a vertical line through g^* since

$$dv/dg = -(g_1 + 2a_1 g) = 0$$

Cubbin and Leech (1986, p.126) suggested that estimating the valuation frontier along with the expansion path may provide an estimate of λ_1. Unfortunately, the valuation frontier, as stated above, and the expansion path do not constitute an identifiable system of equations. It is not surprising that the empirical work of Cubbin and Leech (1986) did not yield any meaningful estimates of either of these equations.

Working with certain dynamic formulations Chow (1981), and Hughes-Hallet and Ancot (1982) considered estimation

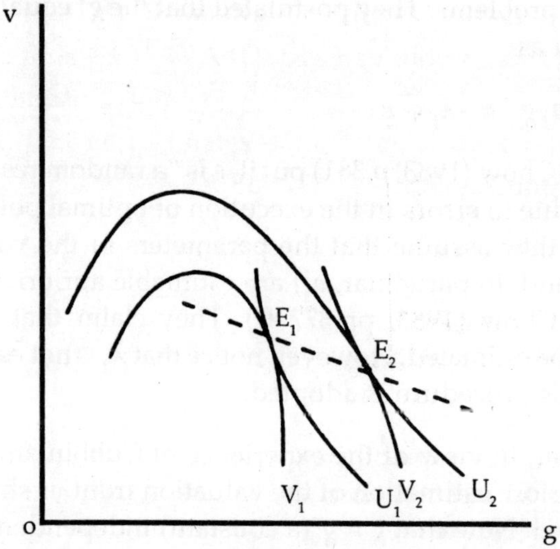

Figure 2.1 (a)

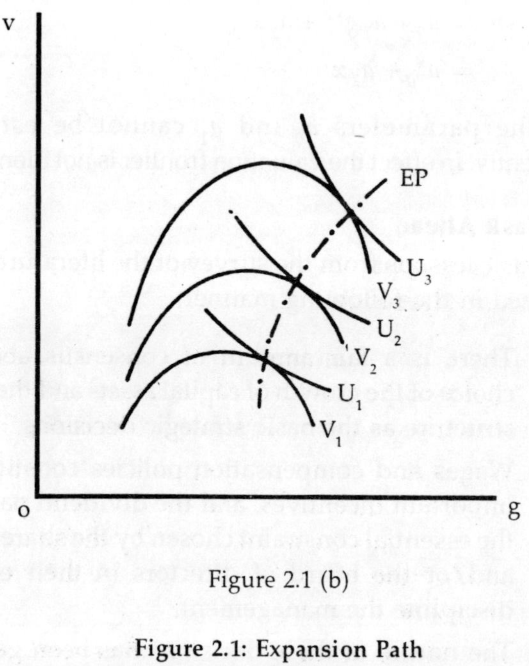

Figure 2.1 (b)

Figure 2.1: Expansion Path

in similar problems. They postulated that the g^* equation can be written as

$$2a_1 g = -\lambda_1 + \varepsilon$$

Where, as Chow (1983, p.381) put it, ε is "a random residual... which is due to errors in the execution of optimal policy." In addition, they assume that the parameters of the valuation frontier (and, in particular, a_1) are estimable apriori. See, for instance, Chow (1983, pp.377 ff). They claim that λ_1 can therefore be estimated. However, notice that λ_2 is not estimable even if this procedure is adopted.

Further, in view of the experience of Cubbin and Leech (1986), apriori estimation of the valuation frontier should be reexamined. Note that $g = g^*$(a constant) independent of the values of x and y. Hence, the valuation frontier can be written as

$$\begin{aligned} v &= a_0 + a_1 g^{*2} + a_2 x \\ &= a^*_0 + a_2 x \end{aligned}$$

so that the parameters a_0 and a_1 cannot be estimated independently. In effect the valuation frontier is not identifiable.

2.6 The Task Ahead

The basic lessons from the survey of the literature can be summarized in the following manner.

(a) There is a fair amount of consensus about the choice of the growth of capital assets and the capital structure as the basic strategic decisions.

(b) Wages and compensation policies constitute the important incentives, and the dividend payments the essential constraint chosen by the shareholders and/or the board of directors in their effort to discipline the management.

(c) The nature of these decisions has been generally

described without reference to any synthetic decision model. Similarly, the hypotheses concerning managerial discretion are only loosely articulated.

(d) There is a severe problem of identification while estimating such models. This problem has been intractable so far.

With this in perspective the rest of the study proceeds as follows:

(i) Set up a theoretically justifiable specification of the functional form for the valuation frontier, viz.,

$$v = v(g, \theta, x)$$

and the preference function

$$u = u(v, y)$$

(ii) In particular, the specification should be such that

$$g = g(x, y)$$
$$\theta = \theta(x, y)$$

can be sustained.

(iii) It should be possible to display the bonding effects explicitly.

(iv) The economic basis for the resolution of the identification problem should be investigated. The estimation method should be developed with this in perspective. Meaningful empirical work regarding managerial preferences can begin only if these tasks can be accomplished.

NOTES

1. Two distinct approaches are available. Demsetz and Lehn (1985), Jensen and Warner (1988), and Leech and Leahy (1991), utilize measures like the percentage of shareholding by the largest five or twenty shareholders. On the other hand, Cubbin and

Leech (1983) pointed out that there may be a large group of fairly small shareholders who can form a coalition if and when they perceive such a need.

2. With the passage of time there is a reduction in the ownership concentration since large holding by individuals and families becomes fragmented due to factors like marriage and inheritence. This can result in an eventual loss of control.
3. In some cases the management may not be satisfied with the compensation offered by the shareholders. They will tend to acquire a large enough share of the common stock of the firm to gain control.
4. The cost of financing the capital assets plays an important role in choosing the debt equity ratio. For, when the interest rates on the money market are low and the supply of finances is adequate the management may resort to bond financing to gain some control of the decision making process.
5. According to Hitt and Ireland (1986, p.402) a "distinctive competence is a firm's ability to complete an action in a manner superior to that of its competitors or to apply a skill that competitors lack." Such distinctive competencies can be found in functional areas, e.g., personnel, production, marketing, finance, and so on.
6. Koutsoyiannis (1987), in particular, argued that diversification indicates a desire to utilize resources more efficiently or create markets whereas mergers always indicate a desire to increase monopoly power.
7. Note that the strategy of product diversification can also affect the demand for the products of the firm. Firstly, as a firm undertakes horizontal diversification it becomes more and more difficult for the potential entrants to caliberate the profitability of any one of the seperate products since only a consolidated profit and loss account is available. See, for instance, Hexter (1975). This potential barrier to entry may enable the management of the firm to consolidate its monopoly power. Secondly, Teece (1980, p.232) pointed out that large horizontaly diversified firms may be able to offer greater security to their employees, devise more efficient organizational measures to motivate them, compensate them appropriately, and elicit cooperative behavior. The greater harmony which the process of diversification entails may make the consumer view the firm as a more reliable supplier.
8. Large remuneration, perks and so on can generally be expected when the firm has higher profits. Higher growth rates are neither necessary nor sufficient for this to materialize. In other

words, the operation of the incentive effects is relatively weak. Prestige and power provide a better explanation.

9. The choice of managerial remuneration and other incentives has been considered in much of the organizational economics literature as a problem of redistribution of gains rather than of maximizing the market value of the firm. As Williams (1987, p.30) put it, even in the case of large firms, the capital structure decision will not affect the compensation policies of the management so long as the managers and directors hold a small fraction of the corporate securities. Though these arguments are relevant this position of the Coase theorem makes many untenable assumptions. For details see, Milgrom and Roberts (1992, p.38).
10. However, Barton and Gordon (1987), and Friend and Lang (1988) suggested that the management may decide to limit the debt equity ratio to reduce the nondiversifiable risk inherent in debt financing. For, otherwise, the shareholders who sense the greater bankruptcy risk, may initiate a takover.
11. Basically the argument is that in the case of a crisis the less specific assets can be sold on the market to redeem the debt which is the first charge on the finances of the firm in case of bankruptcy.
12. There is a fairly large amount of literature which considers managerial shareholding as an aspect of the compensation policy. See, for instance, Benston (1985), and Glazer and Israel (1990). In a cross section study of the chemical industry Rao, Rastogi and Saha (1995) included this variable. The results were marginal. For, as Agrawal and Mandelker(1987) remarked the management may feel that their portfolio choices are restricted. In other words the desired bonding effect of managerial shareholding may not materialize. This issue will not be pursued any further in the present study.
13. Lewellen and Huntsman (1970) argued that there is an increased need for efficient decisions when there is a business risk. The workers and the management can be expected to serve the shareholders' interest only if the compensation they receive is a function of the business risk. However, as Garvey and Gaston (1991, p.105) pointed out, the managers would be better inclined to fulfil the implicit contract if they enjoy some discretion. On the whole, the effect of business risk on wage determination is ambiguous. Also see, Garen (1994).
14. Baumol et al (1970, p. 346) is the celebrated empirical evidence for this result. The financing hierarchy however depends upon control and not merely on the costs of finances.

15. One danger in this interpretation is pointed out by Easterbrook (1984, p.656). For, as he argued, an increase in dividends may as well signal disinvestment due to the lack of profitable investment opportunities.
16. They also argued that the shareholders will expect a lower dividend payment as business risk increases. For, suppose they agree to finance the growth of the firm by issuing more common stock. Then their control will be diminished.
17. However, consistently throughout the literature it was found that a ceteris paribus increase in the net cashflows has a positive impact on dividend payments. For one interpretation of this result see Grabowski and Mueller(1972, p.20).
18. In the Indian context Kumar (1984) estimated growth as a function of profits and found a positive relationship. This was interpreted as a confirmation of the Marris model. Unfortunately, neither the choice of profit nor the positive correlation can be considered to be in consonance with the Marris hypothesis.
19. Odagiri (1981, p.40) put this somewhat differently. He argued that as an autonomous team the management attaches much greater importance to long term continuance without any interference. Hence, the takover possibilities of pursuing high growth rates will discourage them from pursuing such objectives.
20. Tests of hypothesis regarding other managerial preferences adopted a similar approach. Studies of Marby and Siders (1967), Edwards (1977), and Mester (1989) provide a representative sample. For an extensive analysis and criticism of these procedures see Rao (1991).
21. The negative relation between v and g is an ex ante property of the preference function. This does not, in itself, imply an ex post negative relationship. In fact, Figure 2.1(b) was deliberately drawn to indicate the possibility of a positive relationship even if the preference function exhibits an ex ante negative correlation. The slope of the expansion is not a conclusive evidence of the Marris hypothesis.

3

Governance Mechanism vs. Implicit Contract

3.1 Theoretical Framework

The analysis of chapter 2 clearly indicates that neither the ex ante approach nor the ex post method of inference has been able to provide a definitive procedure for the identification of the control mechanism operating within the firm.

Reconsider the argument that a coalition of shareholders who own a critical percentage of common stock would try to gain control. From a practical viewpoint the relevant question is: what can be the reason for this? One possible answer is that they will lose the most if the firm is not managed efficiently. Viewed more positively they wish to gain control with the expectation that they can influence the decisions in such a way as to maximize profits or the market value of the firm. However, they do not have an adequate motivation since the cost of exercising control to reduce moral hazard may exceed their share of the resulting gains. This may suggest that the losses due to adverse selection and/or moral hazard can be reduced by shifting the locus of control.

Irrespective of which of the two answers is considered it is clear that the relative choice of the locus of control is functional and dependent on the need to maximize the market value of the capital assets of the firm. If it is possible to ascertain the extent of gains from the control exercised by a controlling coalition of a given size it may still be possible to define the critical size of the control group. The ex ante approach has been ambiguous precisely due to the inability to provide such an answer. Reverting to a functional approach will be more fruitful.

Such an approach should start with the premise that irrespective of the control mechanism in operation adverse selection due to the information asymmetry loss and the attendant moral hazard cannot be completely eliminated. That is, there is a certain amount of reduction in the market value irrespective of the control structure in operation. The decision makers exhibit a tradeoff between the market value of the firm and the preferences or costs they associate with the choices. For, the preference function can take the form

$$u = v + \lambda_1 g + \lambda_2 g\, y$$

The observed choices of g then maximize u subject to the valuation constraint

$$v = v\,(g,\ x)$$

However, note that whatever may be the preference function of the board of directors or the management the actual values of v attained for a given g cannot exceed the value represented by the valuation frontier. Hence, to determine the locus of control, it would be sufficient to compare the valuation under the different control structures. In other words, the estimation of the preference functions is not necessary to examine the locus of control. The details of the comparison on this basis will be outlined in section 3.2.

However, the ex post time series observations of any firm contain information about

(a) a single control structure and its effect on the market value, or
(b) switches in the control structures and the associated

changes in the market value without a clear demarcation regarding the time period at which the switches occured.

Conceptually, there is no possibility of estimating the valuation frontier under both the control structures for each firm.

It is therefore necessary to specify an alternative conceptual basis from which the inference about the choice of the control structure at work can be obtained. This is developed in section 3.3.

As it turns out this procedure has one drawback. It cannot provide any information about the factors which determine the choice of the control mechanism. A practical alternative is outlined in section 3.4.

3.2 Market Value Comparisons

In general, the market value of the capital assets of the firm will be affected by

(a) the product market conditions which the decision makers within the firm cannot influence,
(b) the actual decisions (both strategic and operating) of the firm,
(c) the functioning of the organizational arrangements including the control mechanisms, and
(d) the external control by the capital market and government policies.

Each of these influences will now be examined sequentially.

In a very general sense the product market conditions, as reflected in the market demand exhibited by the consumers, is one of the fundamental determinants of the extent to which value can be added to the capital assets of the firm. Clearly, this process entails an appropriate choice of the strategic decisions and their implementation.

To initiate a study of the effect of the market demand on the value generation process it should be acknowledged that the product market conditions differ both with respect to

(a) the extent to which they can be predicted, and
(b) the firm's ability to adjust to them (as reflected in the costs of frequent adjustments).

In particular, if the market demand and the business risk can be fully anticipated and the firm can adjust its decisions without any significant cost, the market value can still be maximized. On the other hand, if the reduction in the market demand is totally unexpected and there is no flexibility to adjust to it the market value of the firm will be reduced. The intermediate cases also involve some loss in the market value.

In general, the effect of the market conditions on the market value of the firm depends upon

(a) the quantitative and qualitative aspects of the market potential, and
(b) the flexibility of the decision making process of the firm.

Consider the effect on the market value of the firm of a specific choice of the growth of capital assets. Irrespective of the locus of decision making there will be an expectation that when the firm is in its early stages

(a) many profitable opportunities exist,
(b) an increase in the market share can be achieved through growth by diversification,
(c) there is a positive organizational response due to the increase in the opportunities for recruiting new managers, and

(d) the financial constraints are not yet binding.

See, for example, Heal and Silberston (1972, p.138).

In general as Marris (1964, pp.116-117) put it, at low rates of growth acceleration has an efficiency inducing effect which increases the market value of the firm. However, after a certain rate of growth of capital assets there are several adverse effects on the firm. In particular, the following aspects are noteworthy.

(a) On the demand side it is apparent that there are limits on the extent to which the firm can sell more goods while preserving at least a constant rate of profit. See, Marris (1971a, pp.6ff).

(b) The progressive shifting of the demand curve cannot be achieved without incurring ever increasing marketing expenditures. It should be generally expected that there are diminishing returns to such expenditures as the ratio of these expenditures to current sales increases. Marris (1971a, pp.6ff) acknowledged this aspect as well.

(c) Marris (1964, pp.114-115) argued that the growth of capital assets and expansion of the level of production is crucially constrained by the availability of competent managerial personnel who can (i) identify new talent for recruitment, (ii) reorganize the patterns of delegation, and (iii) train the new workforce.

Consequently, the market value of the firm can be expected to increase at lower levels of g reach a maximum and decrease thereafter. See, Figure 3.1.

The influence of an increase in the debt equity ratio on the market value of the firm can be examined in the following manner:

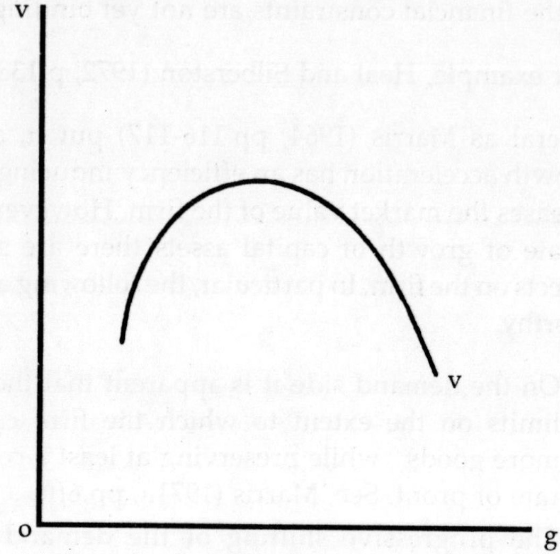

Figure 3.1. Valuation Frontier (*v* and *g*)

(a) In the early stages of growth the firm has many potentially value increasing investments while (i) internally generated finances are inadequate to take advantage of these opportunities, and (ii) there are delays and costs associated with the floatation of new issues. Borrowing from the external sources has the effect of increasing the market value of the firm though the debt equity ratio increases. This may be called the market effect.

(b) One of the consequences of the increase in the debt equity ratio is the recognition by the lenders that there is a reduction in the margin of assets covering their loan. If they feel that this can give rise to the possibility of the firm being unable to compensate them adequately when the product markets are unfavourable they may sell the shares and consequently reduce the share prices and the market value of the firm. This is the asset effect. See, for instance, Marris (1964, p.8).

(c) Following Marris (1964, p.8) and Vickers (1987, pp.63 ff), it should be noted that an increase in the debt equity ratio entails an increase in the market rate of interest. Consequently, there is a more than proportionate increase in the cost of financing new investments as the debt equity ratio increases. The cost effect of leverage is to increase the risk of insolvency for any given probability distribution of earnings. Hence, the market value of the firm will decline.

(d) An increase in the debt equity ratio reduces the control of the outside shareholders. In such a situation, a risk averse management will reduce investments even if profitable opportunities exist. On the other hand, a risk taking management may finance projects which are otherwise marginal. Both these aspects of the control effect tend to reduce the market value of the firm below the potential maximum.

In general, at lower levels of the debt equity ratio, the market effect may outweigh the net effect of the others. This tends to increase the market value of the firm. However, the other three effects are likely to overshadow the market effect when the debt equity ratio crosses a certain threshold. Hence, as in the case with an increase in *g*, the relationship between the market value of the firm and the debt equity ratio is also of the inverted U-shape[1] as in Figure 3.2.

Referring to Figure 3.3 the more important comparison is with respect to the market value of the firm under the alternative organizational mechanisms. The following salient points may be recorded:

(a) Suppose the firm is small initially. In this phase

(i) the information requirements for decision making are low and the board of directors can easily obtain and assimilate the necessary

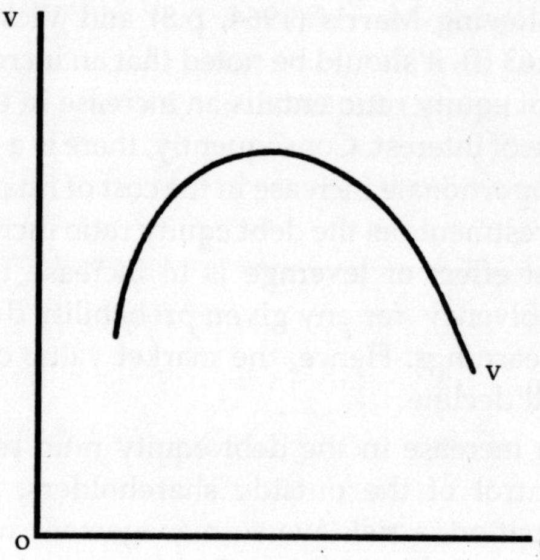

Figure 3.2. Valuation Frontier v and θ

information, and

(ii) the costs associated with the board of directors exercising control are not as yet excessive. Hence, the governance mechanism can effectively eliminate the moral hazard possibilities of implicit contracting and increase the market value of the firm.

(b) As the firm becomes larger there is an information overload on the board of directors. To the extent that losses due to information asymmetry may outweigh the moral hazard inherent in an implicit contract switching to the latter organizational mode may be value increasing.

(c) However, if the growth of the capital assets is fairly high the losses due to managerial discretion may become intolerable. For, in their quest for control, power, and prestige, the management may undertake investment decisions beyond the point where the market value is maximized[2]. The excessive control loss will induce the board of directors to regain control by returning to the governance mechanism. This becomes necessary to the extent that the market for corporate control may not be adequate[3].

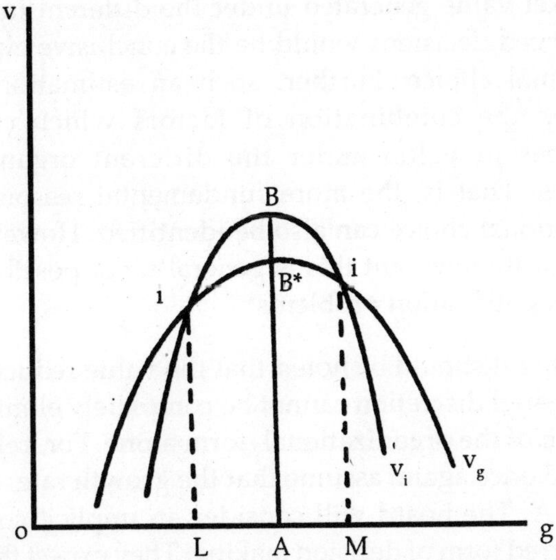

Figure 3.3. Control Mechanism and Market Value

Somewhat more specifically consider the business risk inherent in the product market first. When it is low and the market demand is stable the information requirements are low. As such the board of directors have an advantage in the decision making process. On the other hand, at sufficiently high levels of business risk they have to build up sufficient decision making expertise and information assimilation mechanisms. These costs may outweigh the moral hazard inherent in an implicit contract. The net agency costs may indicate that the implicit contract is more efficient. However, as the business risk increases beyond a certain limit the board loses control primarily due to the lack of information regarding the premises on which the managerial decisions are made. It would perhaps be possible to increase the market value of the firm if they take governance into their hands. A similar argument can be constructed with respect to the financial risk.

This analysis suggests that estimating and comparing the market value generated under the different forms from the observed decisions would be the conclusive evidence of the optimal choice. Further, such an estimation process identifies the combination of factors which cause the differences in value under the different organizational structures. That is, the more fundamental reasons for the organizational choice can also be identified. However, from an empirical viewpoint this is generally not possible due to various identification problems[4].

Further it should be noted that the value reductions due to managerial discretion cannot be completely eliminated by the choice of the organizational form alone. For, referring to Figure 3.3 once again, assume that the growth rate of capital assets is A. The board will consider an implicit contract as the preferred form of decision making. They expect the market value to be AB. However, the management does not feel threatened until AB* is reached. Hence, they will keep the performance just above AB*. Incentives in the form of wages and salaries and/or constraints on dividend payments will be necessary to do better. Though these decisions are almost always under the purview of the board of directors AB may not be attainable even under ideal conditions of bonding[5].

In sum, there is necessity to develop an alternative method to classify the actual organizational choice as a governance mechanism or an implicit contract.

3.3 Advantages and Shortcomings of Different Control Structures

There are certain advantages and shortcomings associated with each of the control systems. Advantage of the prevalance of one of these organizational structures over the other would necessitate (i) estimating the several cost components associated with each of these decisions, and (ii) their relative valuation by the shareholders and the management.

The information asymmetry and adverse selection implicit in the degree of business risk and the extent of control loss and moral hazard reflected by the financial risk have been found to decide the choice of the control mechanism in different situations.

Leech and Leahy (1991) argued that when there is a high degree of business risk, frequent adjustments are required in the deployment of productive assets. The shareholders and the board of directors do not have an advantage in such cases. Control will be generally delegated to the management. Governance mechanism will not maximize the market value of the firm.

When the risks are low the board can make efficient decisions. It will be advantageous to have governance mechanism because the agency costs of achieving the efficient decisions are higher than the addition to the market value.

On the other hand, at sufficiently high levels of business risk the board of directors have to build up sufficient decision making expertise and information assimilation mechanisms. These costs may outweigh the moral hazard inherent in an implicit contract. The net agency costs may indicate that the implicit contract is more efficient.

Though the implicit contractual agreements result in information advantages the management may exhibit a high degree of moral hazard which is difficult to control. See, for instance, Hoskisson and Turk (1990), and Jensen (1993).

However, as the business risk increases beyond a certain limit the board loses control primarily due to the lack of information regarding the premises on which the managerial decisions are made. It would perhaps be possible to increase the market value of the firm if they take governance into their hands. A similar argument can be constructed with respect to the financial risk.

As discussed earlier in the initial phase of the firm the information requirements for decision making are low. The costs associated with the board of directors exercising control are not as yet excessive. The board of directors are efficient enough to make decisions. As the firm becomes larger there is an information overload on the board of directors. To the extent that losses due to information asymmetry may outweigh the moral hazard inherent in an implicit contract switching to the governance mechanism may be value increasing and if the losses are less implicit contract will be advantageous.

However, if the management choses fairly high growth of the capital assets in their quest for control, power, and prestige causing unbearable losses. The excessive control loss will induce the board of directors to regain control by returning to the governance mechanism. This becomes necessary to the extent that the market for corporate control may not be adequate.

Irrespective of which of the two answers is considered it is clear that the advantage of the locus of control is functional and dependent on the need to maximize the market value of the capital assets of the firm.

3.4 The Analytical Procedure

The following notation will be adopted for analytical convenience. Let

x = a vector of product market related variables, government controls and short term decisions of the firm,

c = a vector of long term strategic choices of the board of directors,

y = a vector of incentives and constraints chosen by the board of directors, and

v = market value of the firm.

It should be noted at the outset that the board of directors invariably delegates the implementation of the strategic choices and the operating decisions to the management. It will be assumed that this implicit contract always results in efficient short run decisions. This has two fundamental implications with respect to the choice of the organizational mechanisms.

(a) the board of directors will not take these short run decisions into account while choosing the incentives and constraints. Only the consequences of these decisions, as reflected in the net profits generated in the short run, will be taken into account.

(b) The short run decisions contain important information about the distinctive competencies of the firm. Hence, irrespective of the organizational mechanism and the locus of control, they will have an influence on the long term strategic decisions.

In the general context of strategic decisions it is necessary to acknowledge that there are several other aspects of the specification of the distinctive competencies and competitive advantage. See, for instance, Kay (1995). The approach of the present analysis is somewhat circumscribed. However, it is necessary to maintain the above distinctions even for the limited purpose at hand.

The efficient contracting arguments[6] invariably assume that the shareholders and the board of directors try to achieve the highest market value of the capital assets of the firm. However, the management

(a) derives utility from the market value of the firm only to the extent that it has an influence on the survival of the team,

(b) pursues the goals of power, prestige, and stability of the market share of the firm, and

(c) values the gains, in the form of wages and salaries, perks and stock ownership, which accrue to them. Further the constraint placed (by the board of directors) on the management, in the form of dividend payments, defines the extent of commitment to value maximization expected from the management. It can therefore be expected that the management will take the effort level necessary to achieve the expected efficiency into account while stating its claims regarding the remuneration. That is, the preference function of the management will be

$$u = u\,[v(c, x), c, y]$$

It was observed at the outset that even the board of directors, acting as representative of the shareholders, will place a positive value on c in addition to v. The tradeoff can be exhibited by the preference function

$$u^* = u^*\,[v(c, x), c]$$

The choice of the organizational mechanism must keep these aspects in perspective.

Fundamentally the governance argument proceeds as follows. The shareholders, or the board of directors as their representatives,

(a) observe the market environment,

(b) make the strategic choices, regarding the growth of capital assets and the capital structure, in such a way that the value of the capital assets of the firm can be maximized, and

(c) decide the incentives and constraints that would be necessary to make the management implement their choices.

The maximization of u^* with respect to their choices results in

$$c = c(x)$$

In particular, the growth rate of the capital assets will be determined by

(a) the product market conditions and the business risk,
(b) the short run decisions of the management, such as the marketing and inventory policies, which signal the distinctive competencies of the firm,
(c) the government policy with respect to taxation and working capital finances, and
(d) the availability and the cost of finances.

Similarly, the board of directors may want to increase debt as the residual business risk increases. For,

(a) the risky projects in which they invest may not yield a steady source of internal funds to enable them to undertake further capital formation even when such investment are profitable, and
(b) there are institutional and cost constraints of equity financing. That is, given the decision regarding the growth of capital assets, the capital structure decision depends upon the availability and the costs of different forms of financing.

Hence, in general, the *c* chosen by the board of directors depends only on their appraisal of *x*. However, the board of directors recognizes that the management, which is expected to implement these decisions, will do so efficiently only if the requisite incentives are provided or appropriate constraints are placed on them. Since the management, in its turn, maximizes its preference function *u* given *x* and *c*, it can be inferred they will demand a *y* which satisfies equation

$$y = y(x, c)$$

In other words, the board of directors must accept this

incentive constraint of the management to ensure efficient implementation of their decisions.

Consider the demand for wages and salaries by the management. The following observations are pertinent.

(a) The growth of capital assets chosen by the board is one indicator of the requisite managerial effort.

(b) A high debt equity ratio necessitates greater deligence on the part of the management.

(c) Similarly, an increase in the business and/or financial risk would require greater managerial effort. The claims of the management for higher wages and risk sharing incentives will then be justified. The board of directors must accede to these demands in their efforts to maximize the maiket value of the firm.

However, the dividend constraint becomes necessary because, as Druker (1986, p. 303), and Smith and Watts (1992, p.275) argued, the shareholders consider reneging to be possible whatever may be the salary and compensation schemes offered to the management.

The analysis with respect to the choice of the dividend payout ratio is asymmetric. The above argument suggests that the management determines the limits based on their assesment of the consequences of implementing a given *c*. A substantial portion of the literature on dividends decision takes this position. See, for instance, Rozeff (1982), and Copeland and Weston (1988). However, in the present study it is postulated as a decision of the board of directors since there is an overwhelming evidence as indicated in Lintner (1956), Balasubramaniam (1993), Rao and Sharma (1984) and others. One way of justifying the specification

$$y = y\ (x,\ c)$$

is to suggest that this choice of the management is binding on the board of directors. That is, the argument about who is making the dividend decisions is of only academic interest. Even so, the following analysis indicates that the board of directors may concur with this choice of the dividend payout ratio.

The dividend claims of the shareholders depend on a number of factors. In particular, the following aspects are noteworthy.

(a) When the business risk is high but the long run prospects of the firm, as reflected in their choice of the growth of the capital assets, are good the shareholders may consider it prudent to stabilize the base of the reserves and surpluses on which further borrowing and continuity of the firm depends. Consequently, as noted in Herendeen (1975, p.95), they will reduce their dividend claims.

(b) If the board of directors choose a high debt equity ratio due to the institutional constraints on equity financing they are conscious of the fixed costs implicit in the higher interest payments required. They may take out higher dividends whenever they feel that they will lose substantially if the expected capital gains are not realized. See, for instance, Kort (1990, p.377).

Hence, it can be concluded that in the operation of the governance mechanism

(a) the choice of $c = c(x)$ reflects the potential maximum u^* that can be achieved, and

(b) the y is determined by taking the c and the managerial preferences into account, i.e., $y = y[x, c(x)]$, ensures that the objectives of the board of directors can be realized in practice. This is represented in Figure 3.4(a).

By way of contrast, in the implicit contract, the management would be expected to choose

(a) an appropriate product strategy and the growth of capital assets, and

(b) the capital structure decisions.

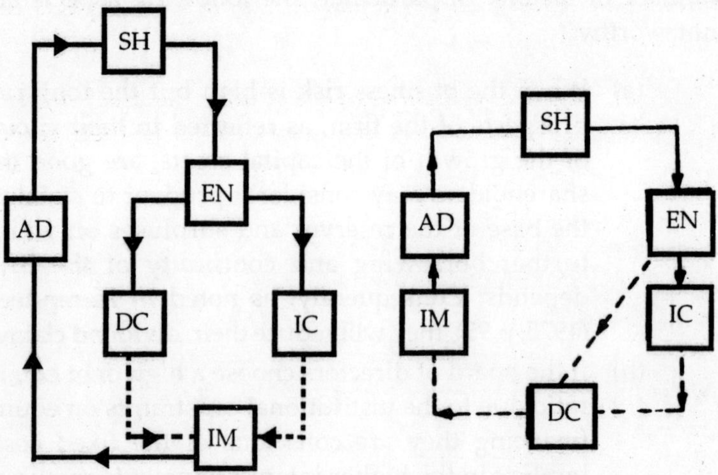

Figure 3.4 (a) Figure 3.4 (b)

Figure 3.4. Governance Mechanism vs. Implicit Contract

SH = Shareholders
EN = Environment
DC = Decisions
IC = Incentives and Constraints
IM = Implementation
AD = Auditing
— = Shareholders' Decisions
---- = The Decision of the Management

A formal approach to the decision making can proceed as follows. The management takes into account the

(a) market conditions external to the firm,
(b) incentives and constraints placed on them, and
(c) effect of their decisions on the market value of the firm.

That is, for every choice of y, of the board of directors, the management chooses c to maximize

$$u = u\,[v\,(c, x), c, y]$$

$$\textit{subject to} \quad v = v\,(c, x)$$

which, as before, defines the market value that can be achieved. Hence, in general,

$$c = c\,(x, y)$$

To encourage the management to choose effort levels and attitudes towards risk in line with their objectives the shareholders would find it necessary to

(a) identify and implement suitable incentive arrangements, and
(b) specify their expectations regarding the share of profits in the form of dividend payments.

In general, given the decision making behavior of the management,

$$\mathrm{c} = \mathrm{c}\,(\mathrm{x}, \mathrm{y}), \text{ and}$$

$$v = v\,[c\,(x, y)\;\; x]$$

Hence, the board of directors, in their quest to maximize u^*, should choose

$$y = y\,(x).$$

The basic differences between this organizational mechanism and the implicit contract is evident from Figure 3.4(b). The following observations are pertinent.

(a) In the implicit contracting framework the decisions regarding the wages and salaries is not a result of the demand from the management. Instead, it is recursively adjusted by the board of directors to entice the management to make value maximizing strategic decisions. Lagged values of c may have some influence on the choice in the context of the governance. However, for the purpose of the present study it will be assumed that the adjustments in y and the responses of the management are instantaneous.

(b) As DeAlessi and Fishe (1987, p.41) remarked, the shareholders may insist on regular dividend payments to reduce the need to monitor managerial decsions. For, the retention of earnings gives the managers an opportunity to divert resources to their advantage even if they continue to make investments which increase the market value of the firm.

(c) The other x variables may have an effect on dividend claims to the extent that they cannot be fully accommodated in the strategic decisions making process.

In sum, the fundamental differences between the two organizational mechanisms can be summarized as follows:

(a) In the implicit contracting approach incentives like wage payments and control devices like the dividends per share determine the managers' choice of the growth of capital assets and the capital structure. The management does not have any such role in the governance framework.

(b) In a governance mechanism it should be expected that strategic changes which the shareholders want to introduce would have an important role in determining the incentives offered to the management. On the other hand, in an implicit contract the strategic decisions will be initiated by the management after taking the wage and incentive fixation into account. Hence, the incentives and constraints will be chosen by the board of directors keeping the business risks in perspective so as to achieve an appropriate sharing of risks and consequent alignment of objectives.

(c) The preference for internal financing of capital assets and the fluctuations in this source of finance induced by the business risk is the motive for debt financing in the governance mechanism. On the other hand, the implicit contracting framework visualizes it as a choice of the managers to indicate their bonding with the shareholders' objectives of maximizing the market value of the firm.

(d) The direction of change in dividends induced by business risk in both the approaches is the same. The only difference is the bonding property in the context of the implicit contract.

Note that, in econometric parlance, this method sought to develop the inference procedure by utilizing a recursive decision structure in order to circumvent the problem of identifying the structural model.

3.5 Factors Underlying the Choices

It has already been pointed out that the deciding factor in the organizational choice is the contribution to value. However, there is no single variable or cause which can explain the variation in value. Hence, it is necessary to identify the combination of its determinants which can explain the choice of the organizational mode. In general, the following types of variables should be taken into account:

- (a) product market related variables, like the business risk and the net profits generated,
- (b) capital market related variables, such as the financial risk and the ownership structure,
- (c) both strategic and operating decisions,
- (d) the incentives offered to the management, and
- (e) the constraints placed on them.

For, these variables determine the value of c which, along with the x variables, determine v.

The identification of the efficient organizational mode then entails (a) a choice of the function of these variables, and (b) the limits L and M between which the implicit contract is in operation. Refer to Figure 3.3.

However, neither of these can be specified on the basis of any theoretical considerations. The choices are mostly an empirical judgement. The following argument is proposed as a workable empirical approximation.

- (a) The preceding analytical procedure already implies that identifying the changes in the organizational choice of a given firm over time is a difficult task. It was not even attempted. Hence, the reasons for the differences in the organizational choice can be identified only through a cross section analysis. In general, the strategic decisions of the firm are based on the
    - (i) market conditions reflected by the net sales and business risk,
    - (ii) distinctive competencies of the firm and its consequences as reflected in the net profits, and
    - (iii) incentives and constraints defined by the board of directors.

In turn, the strategic choices of the growth of capital assets and the debt equity ratio have an impact on

(i) the financial risks, and
(ii) the market value of the capital assets.

It will be assumed that the influence of short run decisions of the firm and the government policy are mostly embodied in

(i) net sales and net profits, and
(ii) the incentives and constraints

and do not have an independent effect. However, the rest of the analysis is valid even if they are considered explicitly. In particular, a cross section sample, of the average values over time of the following six variables, has been considered:

(i) net sales,
(ii) net profits,
(iii) business risk,
(iv) financial risk,
(v) wages incentives, and
(vi) dividend restrictions.

(b) The principal component of these variables corresponding to the largest characteristic root is computed. In general, this captures most of the explanatory power contained in these six variables. It will be assumed that the market value of the firm has an inverted U-shape when this principal component is plotted on the horizontal axis in Figure 3.3. The comparison of the value generated under the different contol structures can now be based on the values of this principal component for different firms. Since the purpose is to identify the best set of variables it is necessary to calculate the first principal component for each of the possible combinations of these variables. The cross section values of the component will have to be computed.

(c) In confirmity with the analysis embodied in Figure 3.3 there are four distinct methods of specifying the limits L and M. This can be defined in the following manner:

(i) Utilizing the classification from the earlier procedure define

(1) A_1 = the lowest value of the principal component among the firms classified as an implicit contract.

(2) A_2 = the highest value of the principal component among the firms classified as an implicit contract.

(3) A_3 = the highest negative value of the principal component among the firms classified as a governance mechanism.

(4) A_4 = the lowest positive value of the principal component among the firms classified as a governance mechanism.

(ii) On the basis of the computed value of the principal component define the organizational choice as an implicit contract if

(1) M_1 : PC is $\geq A_1$ and $\leq A_2$

(2) M_2: PC is $> A_3$ and $< A_4$

(3) M_3: PC is $\geq A_1$ and $< A_4$

(4) M_4: PC is $> A_3$ and $\leq A_2$

Where PC is the value of the principal component.

(d) Compute the organizational choice for each of the firms for each of the methods. Choose the specific method which allows the lowest error of classification. A comparison with the classification already obtained provides an idea about the extent of error of classification[7].

It should be clearly recognized that both these methods are approximate. The error of classification may be due to any of the following reasons:

(a) the time series method used may be inadequate,
(b) the choice of the variables or the principal component as the most suitable criterion for discrimination may be erroneous, and/or
(c) the decision makers within the firm may not make such sensitive calculations but depend on other non-economic considerations leading to the inefficient choices.

However, it is expected that these procedures will provide useful insights regarding the decision process despite certain methodological difficulties.

NOTES

1. In the context of an implicit contract Jensen and Meckling (1976, pp.346 ff) argued that the agency costs are U-shaped. Hence, the value function has the inverted U-shape. Similarly, following Coase (1937) and Williamson (1988) the transaction costs implicit in the operation of the governance mechanism are U-shaped. The value function has the inverted U-shape even in such a context. Even Marris (1964) argued that the value function will be of this form.
2. See, for instance, Marris (1964).
3. This argument is analogus to Coase (1937). For a simple diagrammatic representation see Rao (1989, p.56).
4. These issues are examined extensively in chapter 2 and chapter 4.
5. In a related context Williamson (1964, p.11) pointed out that when the difference B* is small, and the survival of the implicit contract is narrowly bounded, the management would approximate B. The moral hazard will then be low. If, however, BB* is large, the managers may not be forced to initiate efficient action.
6. For a simple presentation see Milgrom and Roberts (1992, pp.45ff).
7. It should be clearly recognized that the limits were not defined in an independent manner. The alternative procedure can only provide some clues regarding the factors underlying the organizational choice defined by the earlier method.

4

Managerial Preferences

4.1 The Issues

Recall from the chapter 2 that the general decision problem of the management[1] can be written in the form

$$maximize \ \ u = u\,(v, g, \theta, y)$$

$$subject\ to \ \ v = v\,(g, \theta, x)$$

It has been acknowledged that based on a solution to this problem, the observed choices of g and θ will be such that

$$g = g\,(x, y)$$

$$\theta = \theta\,(x, y)$$

Hence, the specification of the functional forms of the u and v should sustain this formulation.

However as noted in chapter 2, section 2.4, the specifications adopted in the literature so far could not sustain this requirement. It is therefore necessary to identify a theoretically satisfactory specification of the valuation frontier. This will be taken up in the section 4.2 where the growth decision is considered in isolation. Following Grossman and Hart (1982) the choice of the capital structure may exhibit a bonding effect. This will also be considered explicitly. In essence, this section demonstrates that the economic theory underlying the market valuation of the capital assets of the firm by the shareholders necessitates the choice of a particular functional form for the valuation frontier.

Clearly the decisions of the management depend not only on the valuation frontier but also on the incentives and dividend constraints. Since the latter set of variables do not enter the market valuation they must be influencing the managerial decisions through the preference function. The correct specification of the functional form for the preference function should take this into account. Section 4.3 examines this aspect in detail. In particular, the underlying economic theory suggests that there will be another dimension of the bonding effect. This will be highlighted in the process of choosing an appropriate functional form for the preference function.

Can the changes in the specification be considered to be the only difficulty in the estimation process? It turns out that the estimation methods in vogue cannot resolve the problem of identifying all the parameters of the modified specification. This will be exhibited in section 4.4. Hence, there is a need for an alternative estimation procedure as well.

As it turns out economic theory also suggests a simple method of estimating the parameters of such a model. This fundamental insight is developed in section 4.5. The resulting estimation procedure is amenable to generalization to a wider class of decision problems. Hence, it is outlined in section 4.6. Since the general model can accommodate various specific possibilities some of the important patterns which are relevant to the present study are highlighted in section 4.7.

However, despite the degree of generality achieved in this approach, there will be some practical difficulties in its implementation. They will be highlighted in section 4.8 before embarking upon the details of the empirical exercise.

4.2 Specification of the Valuation Frontier

In general, the valuation frontier is a representation of the expectations of the shareholders with respect to the market value of the capital assets of the firm. As such it depends upon the external market conditions and the strategic choices regarding g and θ.

Given the nature and the extent of the market it was argued in section 3.2 that the valuation frontier would have an inverted U-shape when plotted against g and θ. That is, as Marris (1964, ch.4) pointed out, the market value of the firm depends upon the choice of the expansion policy and the constraint on the supply of finances reflected in a specific choice of the debt equity ratio.

An autonomus change in a market related variable x does not always have an independent effect on v. For, it should be expected that the firm will adjust its strategic decisions depending upon the expected and/or observed changes in x. As such three possible responses from the decision maker can be conceptualized:

(a) They expect the changes in the market demand to be of a long term nature and find that it is possible to adjust g without any significant cost. In such a case the change in x can be fully accommodated by altering g. The effect of a unit change in x on the market value of the firm then depends only on the value of g.

(b) The reduction in the market demand is expected to be temporary but some reduction in g is considered prudent. Some orders for capital equipment, which can be cancelled without incurring any significant cost, will remain underutilized at least over the short run. Consequently, the effect of a unit reduction in g on the market value of the firm would still depend on x. A similar argument holds even for an increase in market demand.

(c) In some cases it is very expensive and impractical to make any changes in the short run. In such a situation the market value of the firm will be affected by the entire change in x whatever may be the value of g.

Hence, in general, the effect of a unit change in g on the market valuation (v) can be represented by

$$a_1^* = a_1 g + a_2 x$$

The general form of the valuation frontier will therefore become[2]

$$\begin{aligned} v &= a_0 + a_1^* g + a_3 z \\ &= a_0 + a_1 g^2 + a_2 g x + a_3 z \qquad (4.1) \end{aligned}$$

Where all the variables which the managers consider very expensive to accommodate have been reclassified as z. That is, if a change in x does not invoke an alteration in g, then x will be labelled as z variable and a_3 will be nonzero while a_1 and $a_2 = 0$. Similarly, if g represents a partial adaptation to the variation in x then $a_3 = 0$ but a_1 and a_2 will not be zero. Finally, if g reflects the changes in x fully then both a_2 and a_3 will be zero. Further, the valuation frontier will be of the inverted U-shape if and only if $a_1 < 0$.

The fundamental advantage of this functional form is that it can sustain the specification

$$g = g(x)$$

if the management maximizes the market value of the firm. Earlier formulations, where gx is not included in the specification, failed to satisfy this requirement. Hence, this is one of the prerequisites of the specification of the valuation frontier.

However, note that the specification of a_1^* does not contain a constant term. The following argument regarding this specification of a_1^* is crucial. Note that, in general, the market valuation of a given g by the shareholders depends upon the market conditions reflected by the value of x. This argument is valid even when it is acknowledged that at least a part of the actual change in g proposed by the management will be contingent upon the expected and/or the actual change in x.

A similar argument holds even with respect to the choice of θ. However, the effects of changes in g and θ on v cannot be entirely independent of each other. In particular, as Grossman and Hart (1982, pp.108-9), Stultz (1990), and Harris and Raviv (1991, pp.306ff) argued, whatever may be the choice of g an increase in the debt equity ratio entails an increase in the interest burden. The ensuing reduction in profit compels the management to maintain the maximum possible efficiency to ensure the survival of the management team. In other words, there will be a necessity to increase the productivity of resource use. This is the bonding effect which tends to increase the market value of the firm as shown in Figure 4.1. That is, the effect of a unit increase in the rate of growth of the capital assets on the market value of the firm depends on the debt equity ratio so that

$$v = a_0 + a_1^* g + a_3 z$$

$$a_1^* = a_1 g + a_2 x + a_4 \theta \qquad (4.2)$$

Where $a_4 > 0$ indicates a bonding effect. This will be designated as the strong bonding effect. In general, the interaction term $g\theta$ will occur in the v equation with a positive sign if there is a bonding effect and with a negative sign if the cost effect is predominant.

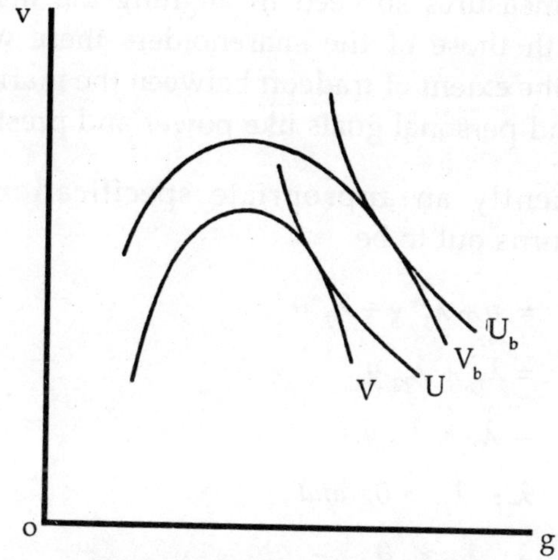

Figure 4.1. Strong Bonding Effect

4.3 The Preference Function

The maintained hypothesis in all the managerial theories of the firm is that the management associates a positive value with the increase in g and/or θ. For, they increase the prestige and the controlling power over the decision making process of the firm.

It is generally postulated that the management would tradeoff the market value of the firm to attain these objectives. Formally the preference function can be written as

$$u = v + \lambda_1{}^* g + \lambda_2{}^* \theta \tag{4.3}$$

where $\lambda_1{}^*, \lambda_2{}^* > 0$

indicates a positive preference for an increase in g or θ.

However, it can be expected that the viability of the management team depends on

(a) the constraints imposed in the form of dividend payments, and
(b) the incentives offered by the board of directors.

If these measures succeed in aligning the managerial objectives with those of the shareholders there will be a reduction in the extent of tradeoff between the market value of the firm and personal goals like power and prestige.

Consequently an appropriate specification of the preferences turns out to be

$$u = v + \lambda_1^* g + \lambda_2^* \theta \qquad (4.4)$$

Where $\lambda_1^* = \lambda_{11} + \lambda_{12}\, y,$

$\lambda_2^* = \lambda_{21} + \lambda_{22}\, y,$

$\lambda_{11}, \lambda_{21} > 0,$ *and*

$\lambda_{12}, \lambda_{22} < 0$

This will be designated as the weak bonding effect. See, Figure 4.2. Note that in the case of any specific firm both the bonding effects may co-exist. This is represented in Figure 4.3.

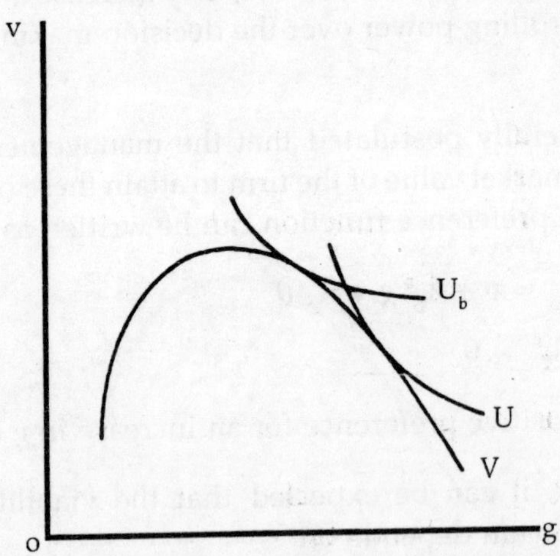

Figure 4.2. Weak Bonding Effect

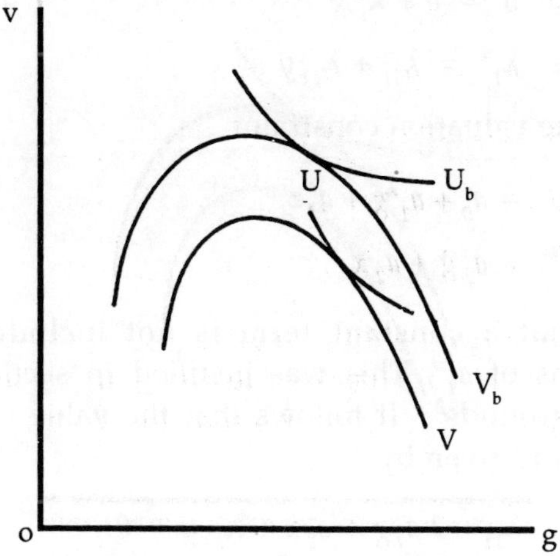

Figure 4.3. Combined Bonding Effects

Suppose the control mechanism is the governance mechanism. Under these conditions the choices of y will not have an independent effect on g and θ unlike the case of the implicit contract. Hence, the notion of the weak bonding effect will not be relevant in such a context. This fundamental distinction must be kept in perspective in the sequel.

It is essential to note that given this specification of the valuation frontier and the preference function the optimal decisions of the management will now be

$$g = g(x, y), \text{ and}$$

$$\theta = \theta(x, y)$$

which is fully in consonance with the theoretical specification of these equations in the literature.

4.4 The Estimation Problem

Consider once again the simple model for expository convenience. The problem of the management can written as

$$\textit{Maximize} \quad u = v + \lambda_1^* g \tag{4.5}$$

$$\text{Where} \quad \lambda_1^* = \lambda_{11} + \lambda_{12}\, y$$

subject to the valuation constraint

$$v = a_0 + a_1^* g + a_3 z \tag{4.6}$$

$$\text{where} \quad a_1^* = a_1 g + a_2 x$$

Note that a constant term is not included in the specifications of a_1^*. This was justified in section 4.2 on theoretical grounds[3]. It follows that the value of g which maximizes u is given by

$$\lambda_{11} + 2\, a_1 g + a_2 x + \lambda_{12}\, y = 0$$

so that

$$g^* = b_1 x + b_{20} + b_{21}\, y \tag{4.7}$$

$$\text{where} \quad b_1 = -\,(a_2/2\, a_1),$$

$$b_{20} = -\,(\lambda_{11}\,/2a_1), \text{ and}$$

$$b_{21} = -\,(\lambda_{12}/2a_1)$$

The resulting expansion path is

$$v = a_0 - a_1 g^2 - \lambda_{11} g - \lambda_{12} g\, y + a_3 z \tag{4.8}$$

so that

$$dv/dg = -\,\lambda_{11} - 2\, a_1 g - \lambda_{12}\, y$$

$$= a_2 x$$

Which does not exclude the possibilty of the expansion path being positively sloped. Hence, a test of the negative slope of the expansion path is not a conclusive evidence of the validity of the Marris (1964) model.

Recall that Cubbin and Leech (1986, p.126) suggested that estimating the valuation frontier along with the expansion path may provide an estimate of λ_{11}. Superficially it would appear that equations (4.6) and (4.8) implied by the alternative specification are identifiable. However, given equation (4.7), both of them contain the same information. This can be represented by the reduced form

$$v = a_0 + a_1 (y^{*2} - x^{*2}) + a_3 z \qquad (4.9)$$

where $x^* = b_1 x,$

$$y^* = b_{20} + b_{21} y$$

This is obtained by noting that

$$g = g(x, y), \text{ and}$$

$$v = v(g, x), \text{ so that}$$

$$v = v[g(x, y), x]$$

is the reduced form of the valuation frontier. In effect, the estimation problem does not involve a simultaneous system of equations. The identification problem encountered in the present context is qualitatively different.

Estimation of a_0, a_1, and a_3 is possible from the above equation only if b_1, b_{20}, and b_{21} can be estimated independently. However, the Cubbin and Leech (1986) procedure does not specify a method of estimating the parameters b_1, b_{20}, and b_{21}. It must be concluded that a_1, and a_2 cannot be estimated. In other words, their method is inadequate even in the context of the alternative specification. The parameters a_1, and a_2 remain under identified unless a procedure for estimating x^*, and y^* is defined.

It can be concluded that there is a need to reconsider the problem of estimation from a different vantagepoint.

4.5 The Correct Procedure

Consider the economic basis underlying the managerial decisions. Let the changes in the market variables (x) and the managerial considerations (y) be given. Firstly, for any change in g which the management conceptualizes it has an idea regarding the likely changes in the market valuation of assets and their level of utility. The optimal choice reflects this information. Hence, it is possible to estimate the parameters b_1, b_{20}, and b_{21} from equation (4.7). However, the management's choice of g does not depend on the position of the valuation frontier (i.e., the value of the parameter a_0). Hence, the parameter a_0 must be estimated from some other sources. However, the valuation frontier is inadequate for this purpose since it postulates the effect on v of an ex ante change in the value of g independent of the changes in x and y. But the observed variations in g are primarily a result of market conditions and the managerial preferences. It is these decisions with respect to g which, in their turn, determine the observed change in the market value of the firm. In general, all the ex post variations in v are along the reduced form specification of the expansion path as represented in equation (4.1). That is, the reduced form specification of the expansion path contains the information about the parameter a_0 though the optimality constraint does not. Rothenberg (1971, pp.584-5) recognized this aspect of the identification problem explicitly.

Returning to equation (4.7) it should be noted that all the parameters of the model will be identifiable only if, for instance, a_1 is estimable. As noted in Rao (1988a,b, and 1994), Rao and Singh (1987, 1990a,b), and Rao, Singh, and Talwar (1991a,b) this is the general problem of estimation in models of this nature. Fortunately, the reduced form specification of the expansion path, represented by equation (4.9) makes a_0, a_1 and a_3 estimable since x^*, and y^* can be estimated from equation (4.7). See Figure 2.1(b). In general, this equation contains information about all the parameters of the model which the optimality constraint does not. No identification problem is encountered in this simple problem if the proposed method of estimation is adopted.

The $\overline{R}^2$ value estimated from the regression for the expansion path can be viewed as a comprehensive measure of the goodness of fit of the overall model of preference since it embodies the information contained in both the equations of the model.

The test of significance will depend on whether or not Chow's assumption is maintained. The estimators will satisfy the conventional t-test if the optimality constraint is taken to be deterministic. However, under Chow's assumption, following Rao (1965, section 6a.2, p.322) each of the estimators will be asymptotically normally distributed. The general case of the next section will clarify the issues further.

4.6 Further Generalization

In the context of corporate control and managerial discretion it was noted that *g* would be only one of the many variables which the management chooses. In general, let

(a) C be a *(p*1)* vector of decisions or the control variables,
(b) X be a *(q*1)* vector of the market related variables which are taken into account in determining C,
(c) Z be a *(s*1)* vector of variables which cannot be accommodated in the decision making process though they have an effect on the market value of the firm, and
(d) *Y* be a *(r *1)* vector of characteristics representing managerial behavior.

Let

$$V = A_0 + C' A_1 C + C' A_2 X + A_3 Z, \text{ and}$$
$$U = V + C' \lambda Y$$

Where C′ is the transpose of C and A_0, A_1, A_2, A_3, and λ are matrices of appropriate dimensions.

Note that the fundamental difference between the

governance mechanism and the implicit contract is that in the former, the Y variable is only a constant whereas in the implicit contract other Y variables, viz., incentives and constraints are also included.

The optimal choice of C would then satisfy the equation

$$2 A_1C + A_2 X + \lambda Y = 0$$

Further, the maximization of U requires A_1 to be negative definite. Hence, the optimal choice of the decisions are governed by the equation

$$C = B_1 X + B_2 Y \tag{4.10}$$

Where $A_2 = -2 A_1 B_1$, *and*

$$\lambda = -2 A_1 B_2$$

However, it is as yet necessary to examine the estimability of the parameters of the expansion path. Based on the argument of Rothenberg (1971) noted earlier, it is necessary to consider the reduced form structure. Rewrite the optimality condition in the form

$$2 A_1C = - A_2X - \lambda Y$$

The expansion path can therefore be written as

$$V = A_0 + (1/2)(C' A_2 X - C'\lambda Y) + A_3 Z, \tag{4.11}$$

Substituting (4.10) into this equation and simplifying yields

$$V = A_0 + (1/2)(X'B'_1A_2X - Y'B'_2\lambda Y) + A_3Z \tag{4.12}$$

For, it is evident that

$$X' B'_1 \lambda Y = Y' B'_2 A_2 X$$

$$= -2\, X'\, B'_1\, A_1\, B_2\, Y$$

It is therefore necessary to estimate A_0, A_2 and λ from the expansion path.

Observe from the equation (4.12), that the parameters appearing in the expansion path are non-linear functions of the parameters A_1, A_2, and λ of the original model. For this case, Rothenberg (1971, pp.585-6), and Magnus and Neudecker (1988, p.337) offer only stiff sufficient conditions for local identification.

However, a rather general necessary and sufficient condition can be developed for the specific problem under consideration. Since A_2 is a $p*q$ matrix and λ is $p*r$ matrix, identifiability of A_2 and λ requires that both B_1X and B_2Y should contain p independent linear combinations of X and Y respectively. A necessary and sufficient condition for this is that

$$p = minimum\ (q, r) \tag{4.13}$$

Hence, all the parameters of the general model are identifiable if and only if this condition is satisfied.

For estimation purposes the reduced form specification of the expansion path turned out to be more efficient. Substituting equation (4.10) in the equation (4.12) it can be verified that the expansion path reduces to

$$V = A_0 + Y'\, B'_2\, A_1\, B_2\, Y - X'\, B'_1\, A_1\, B_1\, X + A_3\, Z \tag{4.14}$$

so that A_1 can be estimated from this equation[4] and A_2 and λ can be calculated from

$$A_2 = -2\, A_1 B_1,\ and$$
$$\lambda = -2\, A_1 B_2.$$

Note that it is generally not possible to seperate all the Z variables from the X and Y variables apriori. A practical approach would be to initially estimate the *C* equations by a stepwise regression procedure and reclassify all the *X* and *Y* variables which do not appear in these equations in the *Z* category.

One further observation is in order. The parameters B_1 and B_2 can be estimated even if the optimality condition is deemed to be deterministic. For example, rewrite

$$C = B_1 X + B_2 Y = B^*X^*$$

Where $B^* = (B_1\ B_2)$

$X^* = (X'\ Y')$

It follows that

$$B^* = (C\ X^{*\prime})\ (X^*\ X^{*\prime})^{-1}$$

So that both B_1 and B_2 are deterministic. In other words, the introduction of randomness into this equation, as suggested by Chow (1988) is redundant though estimation is possible even under that assumption. The final judgement rests with the analyst.

It should be reiterated that this is the most comprehensive specification of an identifiable model of preferences.

4.7 Expected Patterns

Recall that, irrespective of the control mechanism in operation, the estimates obtained from this model contain information about the discretionary use of resources. The differences in the patterns of behavior across firms depend on the

(a) extent of information asymmetry,
(b) degree of business and financial risk,
(c) relative valuation of the different choices by the decision makers, and
(d) efficacy of incentives, and the monitoring mechanisms.

In general, following the revealed preference logic, the choices would reflect

(a) the preferences of decision makers, or
(b) the fact that the constraints are binding.

With these aspects in perspective the following possibilities are noteworthy.

(a) Good market prospects and the flexibility of the constraints may enable the decision makers to pursue both the objectives of growth and maintaining corporate control even with a high debt equity ratio. Both the g^2 and θ^2 variables will appear in the value function with a negative sign. Similarly, g and θ will appear with positive sign in the preference function.
(b) Suppose the market prospects are good and there is a preference for growth. In the context of the governance mechanism the choice of a high debt equity ratio may be considered as a dilution of control. The management, in an implicit contract framework, may consider the financial risk to be disproportionate to the gains in corporate control. In such a case growth will be restricted in such a way that the choice of θ is in the increasing portion of the valuation frontier. When the implicit contract is in operation it is the financial risks and the expected reduction in market value that puts a limit on the management. In other words, the strong bonding effect will be exhibited by the positive sign on $g\theta$ and/or θ^2 in the valuation frontier.
(c) There are situations in which the current cashflows are low and and financing even the limited growth prospects necessitates debt financing. In such cases there can be a positive preference for θ even if the choice of g is on the increasing portion of the

valuation frontier. This can happen irrespective of the control mechanism in operation.

(d) On occasions the market prospects may not be encouraging and the cost implications of a high debt equity ratio may be a deterrent for further expansion of the capital assets. Under these condition both the choices of g and θ will be on the increasing portion of the valuation frontier. It would be possible to estimate the valuation frontier and the preference function independently. The estimated V function can only represent the expansion path. In addition, the sources of market valuation of assets and the weak bonding effects on managerial preferences will have to be judged from the X and Y variables which remain in the estimated equations.

4.8 Some Practical Difficulties

There are several aspects that should be kept in perspective while operationalizing the model. This is primarily a reflection of the fragmented nature of the research in this area. A few of these aspects will be highlighted in the present section. As such the presentation is not intended to be exhaustive.

Consider an alternative specification of managerial preferences or tradeoff between objectives. It is possible to argue that having gained control the management would be in a position to claim and obtain a share of the market value of the firm as perks. If this is possible, the management may yet maximize the value of the firm. An equivalent formulation would then be for the management to maximize

$$V = A_0 + C' A_1 C + C'A_2 X + A_3 Z + C'\lambda Y$$

and claim $C'\lambda Y$ as payments to themselves. This would be an alternative specification of discretionary managerial behavior[5]. However, at the conceptual level, it is unrealistic to expect the management to obtain a share in the capital gains. The usual specification that they receive a part of the short run profits is more meaningful. Hence, the incentive variables (Y) generally relate to the share of the current profits. If the incentives are in the form of shareholding by the management capital gains accrue as a result of ownership rather then sharing current profits. In such a case the management can be expected to alter their decisions C and accordingly the market value of the firm. The Y variables do not have an independent effect on V. In other words, a movement along the valuation frontier, as postulated in the previous section, is more plausible in comparison to the shift implied by this alternative.

The above argument suggests that there is a more fundamental difficulty in classifying a certain variable as belonging to the X or the Y category. Consider the following examples:

(a) The debt equity ratio choice of the management can be said to have an effect on the cost structure and therefore the market value of the firm. The effect of this C variable is accommodated through $C'A_1C$ in the value function. However, the management associates a positive value to the choice of C independent of its effect on V. For, an increase in the debt equity ratio provides them corporate control and this effect is over and above the variations in V which it entails. This is accounted for by taking one of the Y variables as a constant. The question of treating this as a X or a Y arises only if it is not a decision of the management.

(b) Suppose there is a business risk implicit in the product market conditions. Would the management place a value on this or not? The position taken in the current modelling exercise is that it is a X variable. For, the management knows that such changes have a fundamental bearing on the market value of the firm if they cannot adequately alter their decisions. Such changes impinge on the decision making process of the management indirectly through their effect on the valuation constraint. The management does not have any direct value for such fluctuations in the business risk.

It should be reiterated that, at least in some cases, the classification is a matter of analytical judgement. As of now the analytical procedures do not have the flexibility of allowing a given variable to have the role of both *X* and *Y*.

Changes in the market valuation of the equity capital of the firm and the management preferences are pervasive. From an analytical viewpoint it would be necessary to acknowledge that the parameters of the model are variable; perhaps even random. Rao (1988a) has shown that the estimation techniques can be modified to take this contingency into account. This will not be pursued further in the present study.

NOTES

1. Throughout the rest of the study the expression managerial preferences will be adopted. It should be understood that they represent the preferences of the board of directors in the context of the governance mechanism. The fundamental difference between these two preference functions will be specified in section 4.3 where the weak bonding effect has been examined in detail.
2. An alternative formulation appears plausible. The effect of a unit change in x on v depends on g. This can be represented by $a + \beta g$. The v function then becomes

   $$v = a_0 + (a + \beta g)x$$

   It would be difficult to explain the inclusion of the g^2 term from this perspective. Further, note that the formulation adopted in the text can accommodate the inclusion of x as one of the z variables without altering the estimation procedure developed in the sequel. Hence, this alternative will not be considered any further.

3. It is also a necessity from the viewpoint of estimation. This can be explained as follows. Suppose, to the contrary, that a constant a is included in a_1*. Then the u function contains a term $(\alpha + \lambda_{11}) g$. As a result the value of g which maximizes u contains $(\alpha + \lambda_{11})$. The appearance of α indicates that the corresponding choice of g is necessitated by the market valuation of g whereas the presence of λ_{11} suggests that it is a consequence of the managerial preferences. The identification problem cannot be resolved in the sense that independent effects of these two sources cannot be seperated. It is necessary to specify apriori that either $\alpha = 0$ or $\lambda_{11} = 0$. It is perhaps more realistic to consider α to be zero in the context of a test of the Marris model
4. Note that equation (4.14), instead of equation (4.12), will be utilized in the actual estimation process. It would therefore be reasonable to ask: can the identification condition in equation (4.13) be developed from this? It has not been possible to do this so far For, the only clue available to develop the result is in proposition 18, p.582 of Dhrymes (1970). But the identification conditions have been stated in terms of certain properties of the characteristic roots. This approach is not as yet operationally useful.
5. The important point is that this alternative specification also results in the same choices of C as the model specifed in the previous section. To that extent the two specifications are equivalent. The differences between them must be examined from a different vantagepoint before making a choice.

5

Measurement of Variables

5.1 The Nature of the Empirical Work

The basic claims of Chapters 3 and 4 are that the alternative methods proposed therein are

(a) theoretically superior to the existing literature, and
(b) more amenable to empirical implementation.

Hence, the rest of the present study is devoted to an illustrative empirical exercise. It is to be expected that such an exercise not only validates the methodological claims but also provides more satisfactory answers to the questions posed in Chapter 1 in comparison to what has been possible so far.

The present study relates to the chemical industry in the corporate sector. It is based on the time series data for 27 firms[1]. The basic sources of the data are the balance sheets, and the profit and loss accounts of these companies as published in the various issues of the Bombay Stock Exchange official directory.

No particular sampling design was used in selecting the firms. Instead, all the firms, for which at least 20 years of data between 1967-1994 was available for all the relevant variables, were included.

Section 5.2 describes the measurement of variables and

the rationale for the specific choices adopted. The finer details are reported in Appendix-C. Section 5.3 outlines certain precautions that must be kept in perspective while interpreting the empirical results.

5.2 The Variables

On the basis of the theoretical specification of the model in the preceding chapter the variables[2] can be broadly categorized in the following manner:

(a) The variable representing the market value of the firm,

(b) Decision variables,

(c) Market related variables,

(d) Operating decisions,

(e) Government policy variables,

(f) Incentives and constraints,

(g) Z variables.

The definitions and measurement of these variables will now be considered sequentially.

5.2.1 *The Market Value of the Firm*

For all practical purposes the market value of the firm represents the expected value of the capital assets of the firm at any given point of time. It can be ascertained from the following conceptual experiment.

Suppose there is a takeover threat at any point of time. The market price offered for the common stock of the firm depends upon the assessed market potential and the value of the capital assets. However, the total value of the assets should be equal to the total liabilities. Hence, the market value of the firm is computed by taking all the liabilities into account[3]. In particular, the raider should pay off the debentures and long term loans in the first instance. The next priority is to pay the preference shareholders. The market price offered for the common stock accounts for the remaining market value. For, note that, as reported in the stock exchange official directory, the book value of the firm makes an allowance for the shareholders' reserves. Hence, this item of liabilities is not included seperately in the calculation of the market value of the firm. For all practical purposes this approach provides a good enough proxy for the market valuation of the physical capital of the firm if the capital market adequately reflects the financial wellbeing of the firm. Hence, the market value of the firm is estimated in the following manner:

MAVA = Market value of the firm (Rs. crores)
= (valuation ratio)*(book value of common stock) +preference capital + long term loans + debentures

where, valuation ratio = market price/book value of a unit of common stock

5.2.2 *Decision Variables*

It was argued in section 2.3 of chapter 2 that the most important long term decisions are the debt equity ratio and the rate of growth of capital assets. In general, the management can choose these variables in such a way that they can gain control over the utilization of the capital assets of the firm. Following Turnovsky (1970, p.1065) the debt equity ratio was defined in terms of the book value rather than the market value. That is,

DEBT = Debt equity ratio
= (long term loans + debentures)/(equity capital + preference capital + reserves and surpluses)

The growth rate of the capital assets is measured by

GRTH = Growth rate of the capital assets
= [net fixed assets at t - net fixed assets at (t-1)]/[net fixed assets at (t-1)]

expressed as a percentage, where,

t = a specific time period

5.2.3 *Market Related variables*

This group consists of variables which represent the market environment. These variables have been designated as the *X* variables in the analysis.

Following Whittington (1988, p.250), and Lyles and Schwenk (1992, pp.157ff) it can be argued that it is not easy to define the market environment the way it is. For, it can be assessed only through the perception of the shareholders and/or the management which has been built up over time in the form of distinctive competencies. That is, the observed values must be used as a proxy for the ex ante expectations. Hence, the market related variables have been caliberated in the following manner.

Net sales[4] constitute the effective volume of business on which the profit or loss accrues. At any one point of time it represents the expected market conditions. Over the years it embodies the information concerning the expectations regarding the future market trend, its stability, and the distinctive competencies of the firm. It was defined as

NSAL = Net sales (Rs. crores)

This has also been used as proxy for the size of the firm[5].

Business risk is the other major variable representing the market environment. Turnovsky (1970, p.1064), and Vickers (1987, pp.162-3) characterize the business risk as the variablity in the demand for the different products of the firm when the product markets are uncertain. For purposes of the present study it has been defined in terms of the degree of instability in the firm's net operating income[6]:

BSRI = Business risk

= absolute value of [net sales at t - net sales at (t-1)/net sale at t]

Turnovsky (1970) considers the financial risk as an additional risk to the stockholders as a consequence of the use of borrowed funds. In general, it should be noted that an increase in the debt equity ratio increases the rate of interest on borrowed funds. This creates a more than proportionate increase in the interest payments. A larger proportion of the net sales will then be necessary to cover the interest obligations since the interest payments are, for all practical purposes, a fixed cost. An uncertain product market aggravates the financial risk implicit in the choice of a high debt equity ratio[7]. The financial risk[8] is therefore measured by

FIRI = Financial risk
= interest payments/net sales

5.2.4 Operating Decisions

Once the fixed assets are in place, their short term utilization determines the extent to which profits can be generated and the potential realized. In other words, the short term decisions determine the profits and the contribution to the market value of the firm along with the external market conditions. In general, the following three variables can be defined on the basis of the available data:

INSA = Inventory to sales ratio
= end of period inventory/net sales

The expectation is that inventory holdings result in some costs for the firm if they are unintended.

CAPA = Capacity utilization
= net sales/(net fixed assets + current assets)

This ratio reflects the firm's distinctive competencies which enable it to convert the market opportunities into net sales through an appropriate utilization of the available capital assets.

It is evident that neither of these variables can comprehensively reflect the cost effects of all the short term operating decisions. The variable[9]

NPRO = Net profits (Rs. crores)

has been included to capture these residual effects[10].

5.2.5 Government Policy Variables

Generally the government policy is one of the dimensions of the atmosphere in which the firm operates. As such it can be argued that the variables reflecting the government policy are *X* variables. In other words, their effect on the shareholders' valuation of the market value of the firm will be the main reason for the changes in the strategic decisions of the management. The following variables have been treated as policy variables.

Short term liquidity problems for financing working capital have been well documented in the context of the Indian corporate sector. See, for example, Dixit (1992). It can be expected that the working capital shortage reduces the production potential and makes it difficult to convert fixed assets to profits. The liquidity position is measured by

LIQD = Liquidity ratio
= current assets / current liabilities

The other important variable is the corporate profit tax rate. It is defined as

TAXT = Taxation rate
= provision for taxation / pre tax profit

5.2.6 Incentives and Constraints

Incentives[11] and constraints are the most important set

of *Y* variables which affect the decision making process of the management. These variables have been operationalized as follows.

Wages and salaries is one of the elements of the compensation package offered to the management. Its impact on the decision making can be reflected by

WASA = wages and salaries/cost of goods sold

As DeAlessi and Fishe (1987, p.41) put it, the shareholders may insist on regular dividend payments to reduce the need to monitor the management. For, the retention of earnings gives the managers an opportunity to divert resources to their advantage even if they continue to make investments which increase the market value of the firm. The conventional measure of such a constraint on the management is

DIND = dividend per share (in Rs.)

5.2.7 Z Variables

Basically all the *X* and *Y* variables mentioned above can qualify as *Z* variables. For, as specified in section 4.2, all the variables which the decision makers consider very expensive to adjust to in their decision making have been classified as *Z* variables.

However, one observation is noteworthy. The specification of the valuation frontier clearly indicates that a particular *X* variable which does not affect the *C* decision would nevertheless have an effect on the market value of the firm. Can a similar hypothesis be maintained with respect to the *Y* variables?

Consider the WASA variable. Assume that the management is unwilling to exhibit any weak bonding effect in their decision making. Even so, an increase in the WASA represents a cost to the firm and has an effect on the market value of the firm. The shareholders can be expected to view the increase in WASA from this vantagepoint especially in situations where the weak bonding effect is not discernible. On the other hand, they may not consider it as value reducing if a weak bonding effect is exhibited.

Similarly, assume that an increase in DIND does not result in the expected bonding effect. Then the shareholders may feel that the reductions in the cashflows available for capital formation and the associated capital structure may reduce the market value of the firm. In other words, there is a conceptual possibility that the *Y* variables have the role of *Z* variables in the valuation frontier in the absence of weak bonding effects.

5.3 Summing Up

Table 5.1 provides a summary view of all the variables used in the analysis.

The following observations must be kept in perspective before proceeding to the interpretation of the empirical results:

(a) The size effects may be captured either by NSAL or NPRO. In some initial rounds the net fixed assets was also included as a size measure. In general, it is rather difficult to determine the conditions under which one of these is more important than the others.

(b) In general, it is difficult to specify all the relevant operating decisions. Omissions may reduce the explanatory power of the model. There is a certain amount of overlap in the use of CAPA, NPRO, and NSAL. They may enter the estimated equations either through the market effects or the cost effects of operating decisions. Some judgement is inevitable in the interpretation of the results.

TABLE 5.1

LABELS OF THE VARIABLES

S.No.	*Variable*	*Abbreviation*
1.	Market value of the firm	MAVA
2.	Debt equity ratio	DEBT
3.	Rate of growth of capital assets	GRTH
4.	Net sales	NSAL
5.	Business risk	BSRI
6.	Financial risk	FIRI
7.	Inventory to sales ratio	INSA
8.	Capacity utilization	CAPA
9.	Net profit	NPRO
10.	Liqiudity ratio	LIQD
11.	Taxation rate	TAXT
12.	Wages and salaries to cost of goods sold	WASA
13.	Dividends per share	DIND

(c) It was argued that the decision makers of most of the firms do not value both growth and capital structure. Stated differently, they operate on the increasing portion of the valuation frontier with respect to at least one of these decisions. Suppose, DEBT is the variable under consideration in a specific context. It is therefore expected that DEBT and/or $DEBT^2$ will apppear in the valuation frontier with a positive sign. The possibility was tested explicitly by including these two as possible *Z* variables.

These basic precautions were necessary while carrying out the conceptual exercise.

NOTES

1. The list of the firms is presented in appendix-A.

2. For purposes of ready reference appendix B reproduces the definitions of the variables from the explanatory notes of the stock exchange directory.

3. Current liabilities have not been taken into account for two reasons:
   (a) it would be unusual for short term creditors to have a claim on the capital assets, and
   (b) it is generally expected that current assets are sufficiently large and adequate to pay the current liabilities.
4. It can be argued that the shareholders may only have the information about gross sales while valuing the capital assets. However, total sales include the goods returned, allowances, and discount in addition to operating income. Hence, net sales may be the more appropriate variable in the valuation function.
5. Strictly speaking the literature indicates the importance of the size effect on the compensation policy alone. In such a context net sales, rather than net fixed assets, would be a better proxy for the size of the firm.
6. Note that conceptually a measure of the variance of net sales at time t would be the appropriate measure of business risk. Since this cannot be measured in a convenient fashion the procedure adopted is the best approximation.
7. It is unreasonable to expect the debt equity ratio to serve the role of financial risk.. For, the latter is a flow measure for each interval of time. On the other hand, the debt equity ratio captures the bankruptcy risk involved in the liquidation of the capital assets at a point of time. Even in the long run, a high debt equity ratio captures the financial risk given the expected product market conditions. It cannot indicate the nature of the product market conditions per se.
8. An alternative measure of financial risk is FIRI = interest payment/gross profit. This would have been a better choice because interest is paid from the gross profit. But there is a practical difficulty with this measure. Suppose, the gross profit is negative . Then, even if the interest burden is low and the ratio is low it does not mean that the firm is not facing a financial risk. Instead, the firm has to either divert money from its reserves and surpluses account or borrow money for the payment of interest. On the other hand, net sales cannot be negative.
9. Gross profit does not indicate the performance of a company which is relevant to the valuation of the capital assets. For,

suppose, the debt is large. Then a large proportion of earnings is absorbed in interest payments and has the effect of restricting value adding investments. In general, the shareholders should consider net profits as the more appropriate variable in their valuation process.

10. In some cases this may displace the NSAL if the market effect is not prominent.
11. Managerial shareholding has been considered as an incentive provided to the management for the alignment of their objectives with those of the shareholders. It has not been included in the present study due to the non-availability of the data on a time series basis. Rao, Rastogi, and Saha (1995) included this variable in their cross section study.

6

Corporate Governance

6.1 The Scope

The primary aim of the empirical work reported in this chapter is to examine the nature of the control mechanism in operation in each of the firms in the chemical industry for which relevant data was assembled. Following the methodology of chapter 3 both the alternative models of the control mechanism were estimated initially. Given the choice of the *X* and *Y* variables the specification of the two models can be summarized as follows:

(a) Governance Mechanism

DEBT and GRTH = f (NSAL, BSRI, FIRI, INSA, CAPA, NPRO, LIQD, TAXT)

WASA and DIND = f (BSRI, FIRI, NPRO, TAXT, DEBT, GRTH)

(b) Implicit Contract

DEBT and GRTH = f (NSAL, BSRI, FIRI, INSA, CAPA, NPRO, LIQD, TAXT, WASA, DIND)

WASA and DIND = f (BSRI, FIRI, NPRO, TAXT)

In particular, if the capital structure decision is a governance mechanism,

(a) the WASA and DIND variables will not appear in

the DEBT and GRTH equations, whereas

(b) the strategy variables, viz , DEBT and GRTH, will modify the choice of incentives.

On the other hand, in an implicit contract

(a) the WASA and DIND variables appear in the equation for the strategic decisions, but

(b) the strategy variables will not determine the choice of WASA and DIND.

Utilizing the estimated equations as a basis for classifying the control mechanism as a governance structure or an implicit contract it was found that six firms have the governance mechanism while the rest adopt the implicit contract. The principal component approach is then adopted to identify the proximate reasons for the specific choice of the control mechanism.

The estimated equations exhibited certain general trends irrespective of the control mechanism in operation. These results are reported in section 6.2. Section 6.3 presents the results for the firms whose control structure was identified as a governance mechanism. The salient features of firms which adopt the implicit contract framework have been described in section 6.4. Section 6.5 summarizes the efforts to identify the reasons for the observed choices of the control mechanism. Since all the firms cannot be expected to adopt a uniform reasoning in their choice of the control mechanism an attempt was also made to explain the discrepancies between the two methods. Section 6.6 provides a broad summary of the results.

6.2 General Features

The following general observations may be recorded. Irrespective of the nature of the organizational structure the decision making of most firms exhibits the following features:

(a) The firms determine the optimal level of their capital assets by taking into account the long run opportunities and strengths rather than short term market fluctuations and uncertainties. This is indicated by the negligible influence of BSRI on GRTH. However, they are somewhat sensitive to financial risks. For, FIRI appears in the GRTH equation at least in some cases.

(b) In consonance with the pecking order theory of corporate finance there is a general preference for internal sources of funds to finance capital investments. However, when business opportunities arise and internal finances are inadequate they are taken advantage of by resorting to debt finance. For, DEBT increases with BSRI in several cases.

6.3 The Governance Mechanism

Consider the six firms which are governed by the board of directors. Tables 6.1 and 6.2 report the estimated equations for DEBT and GRTH respectively. Tables 6.3 and 6.4 contain the details regarding the estimated WASA and DIND equations. The following observations are pertinent.

(a) Tables 6.4 and 6.5 indicate that neither DEBT nor GRTH appeared in the WASA and DIND equations for Arl, Poly, and Ralli. The major reasons for this may be the time lags in the decision process which could not be estimated satisfactorily. However, referring to Tables 6.1 and 6.2, the equations for DEBT and GRTH did not contain WASA and DIND. It was therefore necessary to classify their organizational structure as a governance mechanism.

(b) Table 6.1 indicates that the DEBT equation depends on the availability of internal finances, the risks associated with the product market, and the distinctive competencies of a firm. The following features are noteworthy.

TABLE 6.1

The Estimated DEBT Equation (Governance Mechanism)

Firm	*CONS*	*NPRO*	*BSRI*	*TAXT*	*CAPA*	*INSA*	$\overline{R}^2$
Alb	0.46	-0.13	—	-0.43	—	—	0.82
	(0.053)*	(0.051)		(0.13)			
Arl	4.34	—	—	—	-2.03	-4.79	0.54
	(1.62)				(1.14)	(1.77)	
Glaxo	0.83	—	—	—	—	-2.21	0.61
	(0.21)					(0.76)	
Poly	1.90	—	1.75	—	-1.36	-1.44	0.86
	(0.38)		(0.45)		(0.27)	(0.50)	
Ralli	1.00	—	—	-1.36	—	—	0.64
	(0.19)			(0.48)			
Union	0.16	—	0.87	—	—	—	0.53
	(0.092)		(0.66)				

*The figures in the Parenthesis are standard errors.

TABLE 6.2

The Estimated GRTH Equation (Governance Mechanism)

Firm	*CONS*	*NSAL*	*NPRO*	*FIRI*	*INSA*	$\overline{R}^2$
Alb	0.84	1.41	—	—	-90.20	0.15
	(19.84)*	(0.76)			(83.10)	
Arl	20.42	2.36	—	-243.28	—	0.47
	(14.57)	(0.77)		(174.40)		
Poly	2.53	0.076	—	—	—	0.43
	(3.91)	(0.029)				
Ralli	34.30	—	—	-723.47	—	0.55
	(14.13)			(489.07)		
Union	-3.23	—	1.12	—	—	0.23
	(3.13)		(0.43)			

* The figures in the Parenthesis are standard errors.

(i) A ceteris paribus increase in the business risk results in

(1) an uncertainty in the cashflows and temporary shortage of internal finances, and

(2) a necessity for larger precautionary inventories and/or an inability to sell the goods produced (as represented by INSA).

(ii) Favourable market conditions and increase in CAPA generate more internal funds and reduce the need for a higher DEBT.

(iii) High corporate profit tax rate reduces the cashflow and, in turn, makes the pursuit of high debt equity ratio undesirable[1].

(c) Table 6.2 demonstrates that there is no satisfactory GRTH equation for Glaxo. Even so the results for the other firms indicate the broad trends. In particular,

(i) the market prospects, as reflected in NSAL and/or INSA, are the major influence on the choice of GRTH,

(ii) the financial risks deter the board from choosing high GRTH, and

(iii) internal finances, though the preferred method of financing, are rarely a constraint on the growth of capital assets.

(d) With respect to the choice of wages and salaries, i.e., incentives, Table 6.3 suggests that the board of directors are compelled to

(i) provide the necessary incentives once they choose higher levels of DEBT and/or GRTH,

(ii) increase wages and salaries when the business risks are high, and

(iii) be cautious about committing to fixed wages and salaries payments when the financial risks and the tax burden increase.

(e) The dividend payments pattern of Poly did not result in any systematic explanation of its determinants. However, referring to Table 6.4, it may be noted that

(i) the Lintner (1956) hypothesis is generally valid since NPRO is significant for most of the firms,

(ii) the board finds the financial risks to be a deterrent in recommending higher DIND, and

(iii) in the case of Glaxo, where there is no systematic explanation of the growth of its capital assets, the board is recommending a higher DIND with increased DEBT to protect the shareholders from the failure to generate the expected capital gains. This result is in consonance with the observation of Kort (1990).

Thus, in general, in the context of the governance mechanism the choice of a higher debt equity ratio and the associated costs induce the board of directors to offer better wages and salaries to the management to ensure bonding. However, the choice of DIND is not influenced by these considerations.

6.4 The Implicit Contract

The implicit contract is the control mechanism in the case of 21 firms. The decision patterns under the implicit contract mechanism are more diverse. The salient points are as follows.

(a) Referring to Table 6.5 the capital structure choice exhibits the following patterns:

(i) The CAPA variable and/or TAXT have a major influence on DEBT for most of the firms. That is, debt financing is reduced whenever internal funds are available. This is in consonance with the pecking order theory of Myers (1984).

TABLE 6.3

The Estimated WASA Equation (Governance Mechanism)

Firm	*CONS*	*DEBT*	*GRTH*	*BSRI*	*FIRI*	*TAXT*	$\overline{R}^2$
Alb	0.083 (0.0075)*	0.043 (0.022)	0.00029 (0.00022)	—	—	—	0.96
Arl	0.10 (0.0087)	—	—	0.053 (0.020)	—	—	0.93
Glaxo	0.31 (0.012)	—	—	—	-4.19 (0.50)	—	0.98
Poly	0.086 (0.0045)	—	—	—	—	-0.016 (0.011)	0.98
Ralli	0.076 (0.0048)	—	—	0.042 (0.024)	—	—	0.98
Union	0.17 (0.0063)	0.036 (0.018)	—	—	—	—	0.99

* The figures in the Parenthesis are standard errors.

TABLE 6.4

The Estimated DIND Equation (Governance Mechanism)

Firm	*CONS*	*DEBT*	*NPRO*	*FIRI*	*TAXT*	$\overline{R}^2$
Alb	3.10 (0.70)*	—	4.75 (0.81)	—	—	0.86
Arl	10.86 (2.31)	—	34.34 (2.48)	-128.34 (29.28)	—	0.93
Glaxo	1.39 (0.13)	1.440 (0.38)	—	—	—	0.94
Ralli	24.28 (8.10)	—	2.36 (0.44)	-527.06 (268.83)	—	0.89
Union	1.63 (0.23)	—	—	—	-0.67 (0.49)	0.88

* The figures in the Parenthesis are standard errors.

TABLE 6.5

The Estimated DEBT Equation (Implicit Contract)

Firm	*CONS*	*NSAL*	*NPRO*	*BSRI*	*TAXT*	*LIQD*	*CAPA*	*INSA*	*WASA*	*DIND*	$\bar{R}^2$
Alem	2.80 (0.66)*	—	—	2.73 (0.65)	-0.75 (0.29)	—	-0.70 (0.31)	—	-9.53 (2.03)	—	0.87
BASF	4.60 (0.52)	—	-0.15 (0.037)	3.86 (0.75)	—	—	-1.91 (0.20)	—	-11.52 (1.66)	—	0.88
Bayer	3.53 (1.02)	—	—	1.81 (0.79)	-1.24 (0.41)	-0.40 (0.18)	-0.95 (0.35)	-3.58 (1.91)	—	—	0.86
Boots	1.82 (0.47)	—	-0.025 (0.020)	—	—	—	—	—	-6.94 (1.79)	—	0.24
Borax	0.91 (0.21)	—	—	—	—	—	-0.12 (0.065)	—	-6.28 (2.03)	—	0.49
Coch	9.19 (2.18)	—	—	6.09 (1.50)	-13.28 (3.52)	—	—	—	-518.85 (183.46)	—	0.74
Color	2.28 (0.34)	—	—	—	-2.02 (0.45)	—	—	-4.01 (1.00)	—	—	0.78
Coro	4.50 (0.61)	-0.0073 (0.0029)	—	—	-2.80 (1.25)	—	—	—	—	-1.06 (0.35)	0.78
DCW	5.68 (0.79)	—	—	—	—	—	-2.34 (0.44)	-7.18 (2.24)	-5.85 (2.39)	—	0.86

TABLE 6.5 (Continued)

Firm	*CONS*	*NSAL*	*NPRO*	*BSRI*	*TAXT*	*LIQD*	*CAPA*	*INSA*	*WASA*	*DIND*	$\overline{R}^2$
Dhm	3.68	—	—	—	—	—	-1.03	—	-14.32	—	0.80
	(0.52)						(0.33)		(2.90)		
Dyes	2.49	—	—	—	-1.12	—	—	-5.21	—	—	0.79
	(0.43)				(0.38)			(1.43)			
Guj	4.60	—	—	1.86	-1.13	—	-4.39	-1.46	—	—	0.95
	(0.58)			(0.54)	(0.38)		(0.51)	(0.91)			
Herd	1.87	—	—	—	-0.83	—	-0.47	-1.28	—	-0.20	0.88
	(0.22)				(0.34)		(0.20)	(0.61)		(0.078)	
IDL	1.04	—	—	—	—	—	-0.39	-1.16	—	-0.11	0.86
	(0.18)						(0.11)	(0.39)		(0.034)	
JLM	1.56	—	—	1.05	-0.76	-0.97	—	—	—	—	0.89
	(0.54)			(0.35)	(0.22)	(0.45)					
Kanor	2.25	—	—	—	-1.20	—	—	—	-6.27	—	0.90
	(0.34)				(0.54)				(2.09)		
NOCIL	2.55	—	—	3.11	-0.22	—	-2.00	—	—	—	0.87
	(0.48)			(0.92)	(0.14)		(0.36)				
Sand	2.41	—	0.071	—	—	—	-0.46	-3.50	-1.75	—	0.80
	(0.67)		(0.031)				(0.19)	(1.02)	(1.23)		
Synth	0.65	—	—	—	—	—	—	—	-3.54	—	0.25
	(0.28)								(2.09)		
Tata	2.52	—	—	1.93	—	—	-2.11	—	-5.64	—	0.87
	(0.37)			(0.80)			(0.40)		(3.02)		
Unic	1.29	—	—	—	-0.35	—	—	-1.95	-2.60	—	0.89
	(0.21)				(0.17)			(0.47)	(1.01)		

*The figures in the parenthesis are standard errors.

(ii) WASA does serve the useful role of making the management bond with the shareholders. The management realizes that an increase in the wages and salaries are a drain on the net cashflows since they are fixed. Consequently, they will restrain themselves from creating a greater interest burden by reducing the debt equity ratio.

(iii) Fluctuations in the product market conditions is the other most important influence on DEBT. The effects of an increase in BSRI on DEBT are the same as in the governance mechanism.

(iv) The deterrent effect of DIND on DEBT is felt only in the case of a few firms whose cashflows are relatively more volatile.

(v) The short term financial strength reflected by LIQD hardly affects the capital structure decision.

(b) The information provided in Table 6.6 does not indicate any systematic variation in the case of Synth regarding the growth of capital assets. The results for the other firms suggest that high GRTH is a result of two factors in a majority of cases:

(i) an improvement in the markets for the products of the firm as reflected in NSAL, and

(ii) the greater availablity of internal finances whenever there is a reduction in the pressure to pay dividends.

The other prominent results are as follows.

(i) In several cases the improvement in the net cashflows, as indicated by a higher NPRO, induced the management to undertake higher investments in capital assets.

(ii) Similarly, an increase in FIRI and the corresponding reductions in the cashflow deter the management from opting for higher growth.

(iii) Though DIND does matter, WASA, as an incentive mechanism to deter managerial discretion, has been more successful.

(iv) BSRI does not have a major influence on GRTH. This is in contrast to the choice of DEBT.

In sum, it can be claimed that the GRTH decision is mostly conditioned by the long term fundamental strengths of the firm such as the product market and internal sources of finances.

However, DEBT financing is resorted to in the short run to accommodate the contingencies arising from the business risk in the product markets.

(c) Table 6.7 suggests that there is no systematic explanation for the choice of WASA in the case of five firms, viz., DCW, Guj, Herd, Sand, and Unic. While fixing WASA as an incentive mechanism the board is sensitive to

(i) the costs of conducting business as reflected in the increase in FIRI and TAXT, and

(ii) the business risks and the necessity to ensure bonding only in a few cases.

(d) The explanation for the changes in the dividend payments, as reflected in Table 6.8, exhibit the expected trends. It was not possible to estimate a systematic DIND equation in the case of Coch. For, the rest of the firms the DIND decisions exhibit the following patterns:

(i) In consonance with the Lintner (1956) proposition, NPRO is the most important determinant of DIND.

TABLE 6.6

The Estimated GRTH Equation (Implicit Contract)

Firm	*CONS*	*NSAL*	*NPRO*	*BSRI*	*FIRI*	*TAXT*	*WASA*	*DIND*	$\bar{R}^2$
Alem	52.55 (15.09)*	0.099 (0.055)	—	—	-890.44 (309.13)	-39.87 (13.30)	—	—	0.50
BASF	22.82 (8.56)	—	—	-50.47 (39.44)	—	—	—	—	0.35
Bayer	19.20 (15.66)	—	2.04 (0.83)	—	—	—	-109.30 (96.90)	—	0.51
Boots	7.12 (4.31)	0.12 (0.099)	—	—	—	—	—	—	0.43
Borax	25.94 (25.50)	—	58.00 (25.58)	—	—	—	—	-4.00 (2.91)	0.15
Coch	1.93 (8.54)	0.02 (0.012)	—	—	—	—	—	—	0.24
Color	37.07 (28.13)	—	3.47 (1.90)	—	—	—	-270.24 (269.06)	—	0.50
Coro	-5.37 (3.71)	0.038 (0.017)	—	—	-63.39 (41.77)	—	—	—	0.40
DCW	24.01 (9.46)	—	—	—	—	—	-93.35 (58.22)	—	0.36
Dhm	46.50 (20.67)	—	—	—	—	—	-156.42 (104.72)	-1.66 (1.24)	0.59

TABLE 6.6 (continued)

Firm	*CONS*	*NSAL*	*NPRO*	*BSRI*	*FIRI*	*TAXT*	*WASA*	*DIND*	$\bar{R}^2$
Dyes	30.50 (8.09)	—	1.12 (0.48)	-40.78 (14.30)	—	—	-217.93 (60.76)	—	0.43
Guj	11.72 (7.86)	0.065 (0.018)	—	—	—	—	—	-0.69 (0.48)	0.58
Herd	15.02 (9.77)	0.13 (0.053)	—	—	—	—	-226.28 (101.59)	—	0.31
IDL	27.31 (2.44)	—	—	—	-364.54 (63.88)	—	—	—	0.79
JLM	19.22 (13.09)	1.03 (0.42)	—	—	-349.12 (249.76)	—	—	-13.65 (6.54)	0.22
Kanor	24.66 (8.85)	—	—	—	-293.67 (155.84)	—	—	—	0.51
NOCIL	5.21 (4.78)	0.056 (0.036)	—	—	—	—	—	-0.71 (0.56)	0.12
Sand	70.07 (20.93)	—	—	—	-282.58 (155.44)	—	-93.96 (49.95)	-28.93 (9.90)	0.48
Tata	43.16 (13.70)	—	1.05 (0.27)	—	—	—	—	-18.24 (7.92)	0.78
Unic	10.78 (0.74)	—	—	—	—	—	—	-0.24 (0.16)	0.16

* The figures in the parenthesis are standard errors.

(ii) The drain on the net cashflow implied by high values of FIRI deters the shareholders from claiming a higher dividend.

On the whole, in the firms where an implicit contract is operating there is

(i) a much greater sensitivity to profit generated and the costs associated with operating decisions in their choice of the capital structure,
(ii) an incentive in the form of wages and salaries to restrain the management from taking the financial risks inherent in the higher levels of DEBT, and
(iii) DIND constraints are not equally effective in restraining management from choosing a higher level of debt. However, they place a constraint on the choice of GRTH due to the managerial preference for internal financing of capital investments.

6.5 Reasons for the Choice of the Control Structure

The above analysis does not as yet indicate the reasons for the choice of one of the organizational forms over the other. To obtain useful information about this aspect the following procedure was adopted:

(a) Construct the average values over time of the salient variables for each firm. The information is summarized in Table 6.9, and
(b) estimate the first principal component using every possible combination of these variables, make the classification on the basis of the four methods outlined in chapter 3, section 3.4, and choose the alternative which results in the lowest number of wrong classifications between the two control structures.

The exercise resulted in the following observations.

TABLE 6.7

The Estimated WASA Equation (Implicit Contract)

Firm	*CONS*	*NPRO*	*BSRI*	*FIRI*	*TAXT*	$\bar{R}^2$
Alem	0.38 (0.031)*	—	—	-4.44 (0.55)	-0.12 (0.030)	0.99
BASF	0.31 (0.039)	—	—	-1.75 (0.67)	-0.023 (0.046)	0.94
Bayer	0.16 (0.017)	—	0.10 (0.054)	—	-0.093 (0.021)	0.98
Boots	0.26 (0.010)	—	—	-0.82 (0.57)	—	0.99
Borax	0.10 (0.0046)	—	—	-0.39 (0.19)	—	0.98
Coch	0.010 (0.0012)	—	—	—	-0.011 (0.0034)	0.78
Color	0.14 (0.0080)	0.0016 (0.0010)	—	—	-0.073 (0.017)	0.99
Coro	0.073 (0.0042)	—	—	—	-0.028 (0.014)	0.95
Dhm	0.15 (0.0051)	—	—	-0.65 (0.13)	—	0.99
Dyes	0.13 (0.0052)	—	—	—	-0.038 (0.015)	0.98
IDL	0.34 (0.013)	—	—	—	-0.16 (0.031)	0.99
JLM	0.17 (0.015)	—	0.18 (0.061)	—	—	0.96
Kanor	0.26 (0.037)	—	—	-1.70 (0.65)	—	0.95
NOCIL	0.070 (0.0061)	—	0.063 (0.029)	—	—	0.96
Synth	0.093 (0.012)	—	0.19 (0.052)	—	—	0.92
Tata	0.15 (0.0059)	—	—	-0.32 (0.069)	—	0.98

* The figures in the parenthesis are standard errors.

TABLE 6.8

The Estimated DIND Equation (Implicit Contract)

Firm	*CONS*	*NPRO*	*BSRI*	*FIRI*	*TAXT*	$\bar{R}^2$
Alem	7.77 (1.23)*	4.99 (1.05)	—	—	—	0.95
BASF	12.08 (1.47)	1.83 (0.55)	—	—	—	0.89
Bayer	18.55 (2.07)	1.67 (0.25)	—	-233.03 (45.04)	—	0.94
Boots	2.05 (0.14)	0.29 (0.029)	—	-25.63 (7.18)	—	0.99
Borax	8.12 (0.67)	5.63 (1.40)	—	—	—	0.96
Color	19.15 (2.96)	2.21 (0.32)	—	-79.37 (40.67)	-13.43 (4.55)	0.98
Coro	1.77 (0.28)	0.063 (0.023)	—	-13.80 (3.19)	—	0.87
DCW	13.85 (5.53)	1.85 (0.38)	29.03 (12.27)	-235.25 (114.74)	—	0.86
Dhm	8.06 (0.51)	0.59 (0.18)	—	—	—	0.98
Dyes	18.86 (3.81)	1.29 (0.36)	—	-105.50 (66.39)	—	0.94
Guj	17.64 (1.48)	0.41 (0.049)	—	-90.16 (16.22)	—	0.97
Herd	1.07 (0.19)	0.32 (0.038)	—	-12.79 (3.37)	—	0.94
IDL	1.02 (0.11)	0.19 (0.040)	—	—	—	0.89
JLM	1.19 (0.26)	2.16 (0.42)	—	-17.61 (5.94)	—	0.96
Kanor	0.71 (0.14)	0.25 (0.097)	—	—	—	0.82
NOCIL	10.70 (1.63)	0.81 (0.057)	—	-66.06 (19.04)	—	0.98

TABLE 6.8 (Continued)

Firm	*CONS*	*NPRO*	*BSRI*	*FIRI*	*TAXT*	$\bar{R}^2$
Sand	1.51 (0.094)	0.12 (0.019)	—	-9.73 (2.39)	—	0.99
Synth	15.88 (3.26)	2.36 (0.44)	—	-292.90 (104.76)	—	0.87
Tata	1.67 (0.075)	0.029 (0.0036)	—	—	—	0.98
Unic	17.07 (5.42)	6.67 (6.36)	—	—	—	0.50

* The figures in the parentheses are standard errors.

(a) The principal component involving BSRI and FIRI, when used in conjunction with method 3 (PC : $\geq A_1$ and $< A_4$) of classification resulted in the minimum number of discrepancies of classification between the two approaches. Table 6.10 contains the summary of the values of the principal component and the classification by the two methods. The estimated principal component was

BSRI + 0.023 FIRI

It can be inferred that the choice of the organizational mechanism is mostly a result of

(i) the extent of business risk and the need to make frequent changes in decisions,

(ii) the costs and value additions implicit in adjusting to it, and

(iii) though the preference of the board to maintain a more direct control when FIRI is high frequent adjustments can be handled efficiently through an implicit contract.

(b) Glaxo and Ralli, which were classified as having a governance mechanism earlier, got the implicit contract categorization in the new method. The rest of the data and the history of the firms revealed the following:

TABLE 6.9

Average Values of Different Variables

Firm	*NSAL*	*NPRO*	*BSRI*	*FIRI*	*WASA*	*DIND*
Alb	10.410	0.445	0.270	0.0221	0.0934	5.216
Alem	37.930	0.929	0.118	0.0407	0.158	12.210
Arl	5.955	0.260	0.285	0.0693	0.118	10.880
BASF	31.850	1.353	0.202	0.0403	0.161	13.820
Bayer	74.530	3.605	0.183	0.0375	0.145	15.840
Boots	32.730	1.815	0.148	0.0162	0.247	2.159
Borax	10.220	0.351	0.164	0.0185	0.0977	10.230
Coch	519.100	13.880	0.338	0.0155	0.00765	19.320
Color	57.550	2.218	0.131	0.0478	0.110	14.770
Coro	120.300	5.695	0.236	0.0597	0.668	1.304
DCW	66.380	2.501	0.152	0.0389	0.156	13.720
Dhm	53.690	2.090	0.138	0.0320	0.111	9.288
Dyes	98.530	1.357	0.143	0.0538	0.117	14.930
Glaxo	153.200	5.620	0.137	0.0196	0.230	1.724
Guj	212.000	18.030	0.194	0.0537	0.0773	20.200
Herd	48.820	2.985	0.254	0.0359	0.0916	1.613
IDL	30.320	1.466	0.153	0.0311	0.272	1.300
JLM	9.146	0.226	0.198	0.0315	0.208	1.128
Kanor	36.010	1.178	0.198	0.0550	0.164	1.013
NOCIL	202.800	13.580	0.170	0.0528	0.0805	18.220
Poly	92.210	5.337	0.207	0.0316	0.0796	18.130
Ralli	223.300	3.442	0.164	0.0285	0.0824	17.380
Sand	62.370	1.642	0.140	0.0337	0.172	1.380
Synth	51.420	1.561	0.160	0.0282	0.124	11.300
Tata	99.480	13.320	0.144	0.0674	0.128	2.081
Union	147.200	5.255	0.118	0.0178	0.177	1.354
Unic	26.940	0.505	0.124	0.0294	0.203	20.280

(i) Glaxo experienced a fairly significant market risk. However, there was no systematic explanation for its growth pattern. It is possible that direct control by the board kept the financial risk under control. The governance mechanism is the more plausible classification.

(ii) Ralli exhibited a high GRTH and moderate levels of business and financial risks. The market prospects have been such that the management is not deterred by high dividend requirements. Similarly, the fixation of wages and salaries is a consequence of managerial performance rather than an incentive mechanism specified apriori. Hence, the implicit contract classification may be more appropriate.

(c) The organization of three firms which were classified as implicit contracts earlier were put into the governance mechanism classification by the new method. They are Coch, Coro, and IDL. The proximate reasons for the discrepancy are the following.

(i) For Coch the history indicates that they had difficulties in maintaining production due to problems of safety and accidents. There was no systematic explanation for the choice of DIND. Similarly, GRTH was not influenced by DIND or WASA. It was classified in the implicit contract group because WASA appeared in the DEBT equation. It is possible that given WASA, the internal flow of funds, and the preference for internal financing of capital assets even the board will exhibit this pattern of behavior. A governance mechanism classification is perhaps more accurate.

(ii) Coro and IDL have similar patterns. Both of them exhibit high business risk. This single factor classified the firms under the governance

TABLE 6.10

Cross Classification by Principal Components

Firm	*PC**	*CRM* +	*CPC***
Alb	0.089	0	0
Alem	- 0.062 [a1]	1	1
Arl	0.11	0	0
BASF	0.022	1	1
Bayer	0.0027	1	1
Boots	-0.033	1	1
Borax	-0.017	1	1
Coch	0.16	1	0[-i]
Color	-0.049	1	1
Coro	0.056	1	0[-i]
DCW	-0.028	1	1
Dhm	-0.043	1	1
Dyes	-0.037	1	1
Glaxo	-0.044	1	1[-g]
Guj	0.014	1	1
Herd	0.074	1	0[-i]
IDL	-0.028	1	1
JLM	0.018	1	1
Kanor	0.018	1	1
NOCIL	-0.010	1	1
Poly	0.027 [a4]	0	0
Ralli	-0.017	0	1[-g]
Sand	-0.040	1	1
Synth	-0.021	1	1
Tata	-0.036	1	1
Union	-0.063	0	0
Unic	-0.057	1	1

PC* - Value of the principal component

CRM+ - Classification by the recursive method

CPC** - Classification using the principal component

a_1 - The value of A_1, a_4 - The value of A_4

-i - wrongly classified as in implicit contract by the recursive method

-g - Wrongly classified as governance by the recursive method.

mechanism in the new method. However, the DEBT decision is affected by DIND. The possibility is that the management has been able to adjust its decisions to the business risk without undue cost. The implicit contract classification is more justifiable.

In general, it can be concluded that the

(a) extent of business and financial risks,
(b) perceptions regarding the extent of adjustment that can be made, and
(c) the relative costs of decision making

determine the choice of the organizational form. The results indicate that the theoretical argument of section 6.1 is empirically valid.

6.6 In Retrospect

The shareholders, or the board of directors, experience

(a) inadequate information, with respect to the market conditions external to the firm, and/or the distinctive competencies of the organization, which restricts them in conceptualizing strategies to convert the available opportunities to their advantage, and
(b) several constraints due to the financial costs and loss of control in devicing organizational mechanisms to implement their strategy. If these risks are sufficiently low the board may keep control for efficient functioning. When the risks increase the optimal organizational arrangement consists of delegating decisions to the group which has the best information to make a specific type of decision. This can have the effect of reducing financial risks in a given market environment. That is, there

is a necessity to involve the management to ensure that

(i) the decisions made are commensurate with the organizational capabilities to execute them, and

(ii) efficiency is maintained at the operational level, i.e., the management bonds with the shareholders' objectives.

If, however, both the information asymmetry and the control loss are significantly high the board may prefer to regain control because the incentive mechnisms and dividend constraints have their limitations in reducing moral hazard.

However, for many firms, it appears that only one of the strategic decisions may be delegated to the management. For example, a competitive product range of the firm may indicate that the marketing managers have the best information regarding new avenues for investments and growth of the capital assets of the firm. However, if the capital structure decision is an implicit contract, power seeking managers may commit the firm to greater financial risks. The board of directors may then regain control with respect to the capital structure decision. On the other hand, for certain product lines in the chemical industry a market can be generated by specific R and D efforts and detailed production management. An implicit contract will not result in an optimal GRTH decision if the management is risk averse. For such firms the board of directors controls the GRTH decision. However, the capital structure decision may be delegated to the management if the market prospects of the new product lines are favourable. A perusal of the estimated equations suggests that there are about as many firms which leave the GRTH decision to the management as those who leave DEBT decision to them. From a methodological viewpoint it may be desirable to follow the Rediker and Seth (1995) argument and undertake a finer classification. This was not attempted in the present study.

NOTE

1. There is a possibility of a high tax rate being viewed as a shield against a high debt equity ratio. For, the increased interest burden is written off against corporate profit tax. In such a case there may be high debt equity ratio by choice. The cost effect of a high debt equity ratio on value may predominate.

7

Corporate Control

7.1 The Nature of Preferences

It has been acknowledged in chapter 1, section 1.3, that discretion is ubiquitous in the decision making process of the firms. The basic objective of this chapter is to present the empirical information about its manifestations and quantitative magnitude. The information so obtained provides some insights into the nature of corporate control.

Following the methodology of chapter 4, section 4.6, the present chapter examines the nature of discretion or the preferences regarding the capital structure and growth decisions for each of the 27 firms in the chemical industry. As noted in chapter 4, section 4.7, the model specification embeds a variety of decision patterns. It is generally not possible to decide the most appropriate pattern for a given firm on apriori reasoning. Hence, computational procedures were designed to check every alternative. The best result, based on the $\overline{R}^2$ values and the condition that $t^2 > 1$ for each of the variables included in the final equation has been selected. Note that the estimated preference function can be either that of the board of directors (shareholders) or the management depending upon the locus of control.

Section 7.2 details the results of the preferences of the shareholders/board of directors. The managerial preferences in the implicit contract have been described in section 7.3.

There is no evidence of any specific managerial preferences in the case of four firms where the locus of control is the implicit contract. For these firms the estimated expansion paths have been described in section 7.4. Section 7.5 presents a comparison and contrast between the preference functions in these two forms of corporate control. Section 7.6 summarizes the results.

7.2 Shareholders' Preferences

Consider the estimated valuation frontier (MAVA) for the firms where the board of directors has the control on the long term decisions, viz., GRTH and DEBT. The estimated MAVA equations for these firms are presented in Tables 7.1 and 7.3. Referring to Table 7.1 it can be observed that four of these firms are GRTH oriented. The following observations about the valuation frontier (GRTH) are pertinent.

(a) Two firms out of this group operate on the increasing portion of the valuation frontier in their choice of DEBT. This is indicated by the appearance of DEBT and/or DEBB in the valuation frontier. There is a general risk aversion to an increase in the financial risk inherent in the capital structure decision. For, GFIRI (GRTH * FIRI) is significant in the other two cases.

(b) The market value of the capital assets is determined by the market demand in the case of three firms in this group. This is reflected by the GNSAL (GRTH * NSAL) variable in this equation. The market conditions were not a major determinant only in the case of Ralli. For, the estimated MAVA equation does not contain GNSAL. In the case of Ralli the appearance of NPRO suggests that the ability to generate profits and finances is the more important determinant of MAVA. In view of these findings it can be inferred that in most cases the product market conditions influence the GRTH decision.

TABLE 7.1

Estimated MAVA (GRTH) Equation - Governance Mechanism

Firm	*Alb*	*Arl*	*Poly*	*Ralli*
CONS	1.96 (1.29)*	6.49 (1.22)	-8.34 (12.90)	-221.0 (73.30)
$GRTH^2$	-0.0039 (0.0015)	-0.0029 (0.00051)	-0.13 (0.047)	-0.059 (0.020)
GNSAL⁺	0.011 (0.0042)	0.014 (0.0024)	0.019 (0.0071)	—
GFIRI	—	-1.35 (0.24)	—	-85.11 (28.88)
GINSA	-0.71 (0.27)	—	—	—
NPRO	—	—	—	5.23 (1.58)
LIQD	—	—	—	279.8 (60.86)
CAPA	0.71 (0.41)	—	—	—
WASA	-20.29 (13.11)	-39.08 (9.90)	—	-653.90 (311.70)
DIND	0.16 (0.062)	—	1.26 (0.75)	—
DEBT	—	—	11.82 (6.96)	—
DEBB	6.34 (1.58)	—	—	—
$\bar{R}^2$	0.50	0.68	0.93	0.88

* The figure in the parenthesis are standard errors.

⁺ The interaction terms in the table are

GNSAL - (GRTH) (NSAL)
GFIRI - (GRTH) (FIRI)
GINSA - (GRTH) (INSA)
DEBB - $(DEBT)^2$

(c) Increase in costs, as reflected in GFIRI and GINSA (GRTH * INSA), almost always have a significant role in determining the market value of the firm and consequently the GRTH decision.

(d) Most of the firms tend to offer a higher WASA to ensure managerial performance commensurate with their expectations though the market value is reduced to a certain extent. Similarly, the board of directors tries to gain the confidence of shareholders by declaring a higher dividend. This is evident from the appearance of DIND in the MAVA equation with a positive sign.

The preference for GRTH indicated in Table 7.2, suggests that these firms have adequate growth prospects and do not as yet experience significant costs in the choice of the capital structure.

TABLE 7.2

λ (GRTH) Estimates - Governance Mechanism

Firm	*Alb*	*Arl*	*Poly*	*Ralli*
GRTH	0.0066	0.12	0.64	4.04
	(0.0025)*	(0.021)	(0.24)	(1.37)

* The figures in the parenthesis are standard errors.

Table 7.3 indicates that the board of directors of two firms considers the GRTH prospects to be promising and are willing to take the risks of higher debt financing while monitoring the costs appropriately. For these firms it appears that

(a) the market conditions, as reflected in NSAL, are the major determinant of the market value of the firm, and

(b) the risk taking behavior indicated by the willingness to use DEBT to finance GRTH, even if it entails a

TABLE 7.3

Estimated MAVA (DEBT) Equation - Governance Mechanism

Firm	*Glaxo*	*Union*
CONS	39.50 (15.40)*	-71.60 (19.10)
DEBT 2	-24.28 (18.55)	-653.00 (287.60)
DBSRI +	—	1101.00 (498.80)
DINSA	-107.30 (81.98)	—
NSAL	0.42 (0.051)	0.40 (0.065)
BSRI	-46.17 (36.76)	—
FIRI	-1090.00 (495.60)	—
TAXT	-46.72 (18.91)	—
DIND	41.99 (9.50)	—
GRTT	—	0.048 (0.018)
$\bar{R}^2$	0.95	0.68

*The figure in the parenthesis are standard errors.
+ The interaction terms in the table are
DBSRI - (DEBT) (BSRI)
DINSA - (DEBT) (INSA)
GRTT - (GRTH) 2

reduction in the market value, is conditioned by a high degree of sensitivity to cost as reflected by the appearance of a number of cost related variables, viz., FIRI, and TAXT, in the MAVA equation.

(c) Union operates on the increasing portion of the valuation frontier in its choice of growth as reflected by GRTT in the MAVA equation.

(d) High DIND declaration to satisfy the shareholders is evident even in these firms.

Table 7.4 indicates that the board of directors of firms have a preference for DEBT.

On the whole, it can be concluded that the board of directors takes into account the market opportunities while expressing a preference for GRTH and the cost factors in the choice of DEBT.

TABLE 7.4

λ (DEBT) Estimates - Governance Mechanism

Firm	*Glaxo*	*Union*
DEBT	40.24 (30.40)*	199.70 (90.420)

* The figures in the parenthesis are standard errors.

7.3 Managerial Preferences

Consider the estimated valuation frontier for the firms where the managers have the control on GRTH and DEBT decisions. Fifteen of these firms are GRTH oriented. The estimated MAVA equations (GRTH) are presented in the Table 7.5. The following observations are pertinent.

(a) Nine firms out of this group operate on the increasing portion of the valuation frontier in their choice of DEBT. This can be inferred from the appearance of DEBT and/or DEBB in the MAVA equation. There is a risk aversion on the part of the management. It is equally appropriate to claim that the managers of these firms exhibit strong bonding effects in the sense of Grossman and Hart (1982). For, a positive sign on DEBT and/or DEBB indicates an upward shift in the valuation frontier due to the productivity effect.

TABLE 7.5

Estimated MAVA (GRTH) Equation - Implicit Contract

Firm	*Bayer*	*Boots*	*Borax*	*Coch*	*Color*	*DCW*	*Guj*	*Herd*
CONS	5.54	10.30	1.36	-82.40	2.43	-0.84	-5.62	8.11
	(3.34)*	(11.80)	(0.62)	(13.30)	(2.25)	(1.40)	(11.10)	(1.91)
$GRTH^2$	-0.16	-0.54	-0.0016	-0.19	-0.020	-0.082	-0.19	-0.039
	(0.020)	(0.036)	(0.00047)	(0.033)	(0.0085)	(0.024)	(0.0084)	(0.0059)
$GNSAL^+$	—	0.13	—	0.0082	—	—	0.025	0.01
		(0.0088)		(0.0014)			(0.0011)	(0.0016)
GNPRO	0.66	—	0.19		0.14	—	—	—
	(0.083)		(0.055)		(0.059)			
GFIRI	—	—	—	—	—	—	—	—
NSAL	0.16	—	—	—	0.19	0.21	—	—
	(0.054)				(0.043)	(0.041)		
NPRO	—	—	—	1.33	—	2.92	—	0.68
				(0.54)		(0.57)		(0.45)
BSRI	—	-39.08	—	—	—	—	—	—
		(25.41)						
FIRI	—	—	—	—	—	—	—	—
TAXT	—	—	—	—	—	—	—	—
LIQD	—	15.41	—	74.49	—	—	—	—
		(7.11)		(16.39)				
WASA	—	—	—	—	—	—	—	—
DIND	—	—	—	—	—	—	—	—
DEBT	—	—	—	—	—	—	25.27	6.18
	—	—	—	—	—	—	(6.58)	(1.53)
DEBB	—	—	—	0.36	11.85	11.62	—	—
				(0.047)	(3.12)	(0.88)		
$\bar{R}^2$	0.95	0.93	0.30	0.99	0.91	0.99	0.96	0.78

TABLE 7.5 (Continued)

Firm	*IDL*	*JLM*	*KANOR*	*NOCIL*	*SAND*	*TATA*	*UNIC*
CONS	5.68 (2.69)	3.51 (0.45)	2.35 (1.79)	17.90 (8.73)	3.20 (1.92)	65.40 (11.10)	13.70 (2.77)
GRTH 2	-0.010 (0.0040)	-0.0050 (0.00071)	-0.016 (0.0045)	-0.16 (0.034)	-0.0065 (0.0052)	-0.20 (0.011)	-0.015 (0.0083)
GNSAL+	—	0.010 (0.0015)	—	0.018 (0.0039)	—	—	—
GNPRO	—	—	—	—	—	0.43 (0.024)	—
GFIRI	-7.35 (2.95)	-3.47 (0.50)	-9.64 (2.65)	—	-3.65 (2.94)	—	—
NSAL	0.21 (0.049)	—	0.19 (0.26)	—	0.13 (0.010)	—	—
NPRO	—	—	—	2.49 (0.53)	—	—	—
BSRI	—	—	—	—	-24.86 (9.30)	—	—
FIRI	—	—	—	—	—	-905.2 (183.50)	—
TAXT	—	—	—	—	—	—	-5.37 (2.36)
LIQD	—	—	—	—	—	—	—
WASA	—	-10.57 (2.13)	—	—	—	—	-42.02 (15.54)
DIND	—	—	2.32 (1.08)	—	—	—	—
DEBT	—	—	—	—	—	—	—
DEBB	—	—	3.54 (0.56)	3.27 (1.33)	8.56 (5.65)	41.53 (7.35)	—
$\overline{R}^2$	0.78	0.78	0.98	0.83	0.90	0.98	0.61

* The figure in the parenthesis are standard errors.

+ The interaction terms in the table are

GNSAL – (GRTH) (NSAL)

GNPRO - (GRTH) (NPRO)

GFIRI - (GRTH) (FIRI)

(b) The shareholder valuation of the GRTH of capital assets is conditioned by market demand in the case of twelve firms in this group as reflected by the appearance of the GNSAL or NSAL variable. It was not a major determinant of MAVA only in the case of Borax, Tata, and Unic. For, the estimated MAVA equations for these firms do not contain either GNSAL or NSAL. The appearance of GNPRO (GRTH * NPRO) for four firms suggests that the shareholders value NPRO in addition to NSAL while evaluating the GRTH decisions of the management. As a result either the product market conditions and/or the availability of free cashflow almost always dictated the GRTH decision of the management since they had a conditioning role in determining the market value of the firm. The only exception is Unic.

(c) The interest burden associated with the choice of the capital structure had an adverse effect on the market value of the firm in only five cases, viz., IDL, JLM, Kanor, Sand, and Tata. Since there is no explicit preference for DEBT it can only be inferred that they exhibited a tendency to over expand though the financial constraints were severe.

(d) The corporate tax policies and the liquidity constraints on working capital rarely had any significant influence on the market value of the firm. The claims of the corporate sector about their deterrent effects are exaggerated.

(e) The management of two firms, viz., Boots and Sand, could not adjust their growth decisions to market uncertainties though the shareholders are valuing this adversely.

(f) Some firms may in fact be choosing higher levels of WASA in comparison to those needed to ensure

TABLE 7.6

λ (GRTH) Estimates - Implicit Contract

Firm	*Bayer*	*Boots*	*Borax*	*Coch*	*Color*	*DCW*	*Guj*	*Herd*	*IDL*	*JLM*	*Kanor*	*NOCIL*	*Sand*	*Tata*	*Unic*
GRTH	6.18	7.68	0.083	0.75	1.45	3.93	4.46	1.17	0.45	0.19	0.31	1.63	0.90	17.69	0.32
	(0.78)*	(0.51)	(0.025)	(0.13)	(0.63)	(1.17)	(0.20)	(0.18)	(0.18)	(0.027)	(0.22)	(0.36)	(0.73)	(0.99)	(0.18)
GWASA+	-35.17	—	—	—	-10.54	-15.26	—	-17.56	—	—	—	—	-1.21	—	—
	(4.43)				(4.59)	(4.55)		(2.67)					(0.98)		
GDIND	—	—	-0.013	—	—	—	-0.26	—	—	-0.14	—	-0.22	-0.37	-7.48	-0.0072
			(0.0038)				(0.012)			(0.019)		(0.049)	(0.30)	(0.42)	(0.0042)

* The figure in the parenthesis are standard errors.

+ The interaction terms in the table are

GWASA - (GRTH) (WASA)

GDIND - (GRTH) (DIND)

bonding. This is reflected by the negative sign on WASA in JLM and Unic.

(g) Atleast in one case, viz., that of Kanor, the shareholders do not view the preference for growth adversely because they claim sufficient dividends.

The estimated preference functions may now be considered in some detail. Referring to Table 7.6 the following features should be noted.

(a) GWASA (GRTH * WASA) appears in the case of five firms. For these firms it can be claimed that the management was restrained from reducing MAVA in their pursuit of GRTH by providing incentives.

(b) However, the management of as many as seven firms feels restrained by the dividend requirements.

These results suggest the occurence of a weak bonding effect in an implicit contract. It may be concluded that dividend restrictions are a more potent control mechanism for aligning managerial objectives with those of the shareholders.

Table 7.7 indicate that the management of only two firms have a preference for DEBT[1]. For these firms it appears that

(a) the market conditions are a major determinant of the market value of the firm as reflected by NSAL,

(b) the cost factors, as reflected in the appearance of DINSA (DEBT * INSA) and DTAXT (DEBT * TAXT) are constraints on the decision making process of the firm, and

(c) the shareholders view the preference for DEBT positively if they feel that the working capital position is satisfactory as reflected by the LIQD.

TABLE 7.7

Estimated MAVA (DEBT) Equation - Implicit Contract

Firm	*Dyes*	*Synth*
CONS	-3.39 (5.52)*	-61.40 (15.30)
$DEBT^2$	-1.78 (0.53)	-134.10 (72.38)
DINSA+	-18.50 (5.55)	—
DTAXT	-3.97 (1.19)	—
NSAL	0.20 (0.0082)	0.42 (0.064)
TAXT	—	-12.12 (6.16)
LIQD	9.58 (5.55)	48.97 (11.87)
$\bar{R}^2$	0.98	0.79

*The figure in the parenthesis are standard errors.
+ The interaction terms in the table are
DTAXT – (DEBT) (TAXT)
DINSA - (DEBT) (INSA)

Table 7.8 which embodies the managerial preference with respect to DEBT indicates that there are weak bonding effects as reflected by DWASA (DEBT × WASA) appearing with a negative sign.

TABLE 7.8

λ (DEBT) Estimates - Implicit Contract

Firm	*Dyes*	*Synth*
DEBT	8.84 (2.61)*	174.10 (93.99)
DWASA+	—	-949.80 (512.70)

*The figure in the parenthesis are standard errors.
+The interaction terms in the table is

DWASA – (DEBT) (WASA)

In general, the DIND constraint is not important when the market conditions are favourable and the management can assure the shareholders of bonding in their choice of high DEBT. Proper incentives in the form of WASA are more important in reinforcing the bonding property.

7.4 Expansion Path

The four firms whose estimated MAVA equations are presented in Table 7.9, did not provide any evidence of managerial preference for GRTH or DEBT. Hence, the estimated equations represent only the expansion path and not the valuation frontier. At best it can be inferred that there are strong bonding effects in these cases (DEBT and/or DEBB appear in these equations except in the case of Dhm) though there are no significant constraints on the market opportunities. Perhaps the management teams of these firms are extremely risk averse.

7.5 A Comparison

In general, the following conclusions emerge from the analysis.

(a) A growth oriented management generally takes the product market conditions and the internal sources of finances into account while choosing GRTH. They avoid excessive debt due to their aversion to increasing the cost of conducting business. This is necessitated by the shareholders' sensitivity to profit generated in addition to the product market conditions. DEBT preferring management is mostly restrained by the cost factors. Risk aversion is a general feature of the managerial attitude in the context of an implicit contract.

(b) The strong bonding effects, as suggested by the Grossman and Hart (1982) hypothesis, occur only in the case of some firms. However, the weak bonding effects considered in the present study

TABLE 7.9
Estimated MAVA Equation - Implicit Contract

Firm	*Alem*	*BASF*	*Coro*	*Dhm*
CONS	8.64 (2.19)*	-1.77 (1.41)	-15.65 (17.88)	26.28 (16.89)
NASL	0.088 (0.0082)	—	0.42 (0.050)	0.27 (0.043)
NPRO	—	6.06 (0.47)	—	—
BSRI	—	—	-43.66 (27.20)	-35.79 (12.6)
FIRI	-166.53 (45.37)	—	—	—
TAXT	-3.99 (1.92)	—	-51.2 (20.42)	—
LIQD	—	—	—	22.27 (4.76)
WASA	—	—	—	-419.50 (127.21)
DIND	—	—	18.50 (6.32)	—
DEBT	—	—	12.60 (3.64)	—
DEBB	3.44 (0.40)	2.93 (0.98)	—	—
$\overline{R}^2$	0.98	0.93	0.94	0.95

*The figures in the parenthesis are standard errors.

are more general. In particular, dividend constraints are far more effective in achieving such bonding when compared to incentive payments.

An attempt can now be made to contrast the performance of the firms under the alternative organizational mechanisms. The salient features are as follows.

(a) when the board of directors delegate decision making responsibility to the management the shareholders monitor both the sales of the firm and the profit generated while determining the share prices and the market value of the capital assets of the firm. By way of contrast the sales generated and the market share of the firm alone are considered when a governance mechanism is in operation.

(b) The implicit contract makes the management risk averse. For, as employees their gains from taking risks are low while they will lose substantially in case of failure. In contrast, the board can take greater financial risks to obtain a better market share even when there is a high business risk. The governance arrangement can more effectively convince the shareholders of the long term prospects.

(c) Risk aversion of the management makes them prefer internal financial sources to finance the growth of the capital assets of the firm. Hence, dividend payment stipulations are the more effective way of ensuring bonding. In contrast the board of directors, operating in a governance mechanism, have greater flexibility in the choice of the capital structure. Internal finances are not a major constraint. However, they are far more sensitive to the cost implications of the choice of DEBT.

(d) In general, the board of directors makes an assessment of
   (i) the market risks and potential,
   (ii) the extent to which the management can be expected to make the requisite decisions, and
   (iii) the implications for financial risks.

They will resort to a governance mechanism only when they feel that managerial decisions would be second best, and/or the costs of achieving the efficient decisions would not be commensurate with the expected addition to the market value.

In sum, both the management and the board of directors assess market risks and prospects as well as the costs associated with the capital structure choice in the decision making process. The primary difference between the two organizational mechanisms is in their degree of relative risk aversion given the market risks. The board of directors retains control whenever they feel that the risk averse management cannot be expected to take advantage of the risky market prospects efficiently. There is no significant evidence of the management seeking or gaining corporate control in an implicit contract.

7.6 Conclusion

The major results of this study are as follows.

(a) The Marris (1964) hypothesis is valid for several firms where an implicit contract is in operation. The management generally pursues the growth objective even if it entails a reduction in the market value of the firm.

(b) There is a fair amount of evidence for the productivity effect of the capital structure decision. In general, the Grossman and Hart (1982) strong bonding hypothesis can be supported. In addition, there are weak bonding effects indicated by the changes in the managerial preferences to incentive constraints.

(c) Value maximization is not necessarily the objective even when the governance mechanism is in operation. Instead it appears that there is a preference to consolidate the market share when confronted with risks in the product markets.

(d) The management is generally more risk averse than the board of directors. Hence, whenever the business risks are significant and the financial costs of converting market potential to asset generation in the firm are high, a governance structure is necessitated to ensure efficient decision making.

In general, the major difference between the board of directors and the management is their willingness to take risks though they both pursue the growth objective. The capital structure decision is dictated by this rather than the desire to obtain corporate control.

NOTE

1. Though the evidence cannot be taken to be conclusive this result suggests that only a small percentage of firms under the implicit contract arrangement indicate any preference for corporate control. By way of contrast the control by the board of directors does not inhibit them from preferring DEBT and committing the firm to higher costs.

8

Summary and Conclusion

8.1 The Problem Recalled

Two issues have been prominent in both financial economics and financial management:

(a) what is the locus of control with respect to strategic long term decisions?, and

(b) what objectives does a specific controlling coalition pursue?

In particular, attempts have been made to examine the extent to which the market value of the firm is reduced while pursuing other objectives. The two standard features of the contract which make this tradeoff possible are

(a) the information asymmetry leading to adverse selection, and

(b) the availability of short term profits which induce discretionary behavior and moral hazard.

The control system of a firm is usually the

(a) market for corporate control,

(b) governance mechanism, or

(c) implicit contract

or a combination of these. In general, these governance structures are important in the context of strategic long term decisions like the growth of capital assets and the capital structure. However, the frequent changes in short term operating decisions necessitate their delegation to the management in the form of an implicit contract.

It is generally expected that the shareholders can achieve the desired coordination through the market for corporate control. However, it has been acknowledged in recent empirical studies that external control via the capital market is inefficient. Consequently, one of the other control structures will be chosen. At best the capital market can ensure contractual performance by offering an alternative in case of reneging.

In a governance mechanism the board of directors examines the alternatives and makes the decisions which the management will be expected to implement. This resembles the functioning of an internal capital market. They may choose an implicit contract as the organizational choice if the information advantages indicate that it will be more efficient. In the implicit contract the shareholders invest their money in the capital assets of the firm and delegate the strategic decisions to the management. Since the management has better information it may exhibit moral hazard which should be curbed to ensure efficiency. Hence, the board of directors devise some monitoring and incentive mechanisms and constraints to discipline the management and ensure bonding.

Ex ante measures like the size of the controlling coalition of shareholders have been generally utilized to determine the locus of control of a given firm. However, it is obvious that the coalition exercises control only in order to increase the market value of the firm. But they do not have the motivation or the resources to ensure maximization since their share of the gains is relatively small. In other words, threshold values of ex ante measures can be defined to demarcate the boundaries of locus of control only if thier relationship to the market value is clearly identified. The functional approach, of examining the generation of value under alternative control structures, is more satisfactory. Adverse selection due to the information loss and the attendent moral hazard usually indicate that there is a certain amount of reduction in the market value of the firm irrespective of the control structure in operation. Usually this is stated in the form of a preference function exhibiting a tradeoff between the market value of the firm and the value associated with the decision variables. For instance, the preference function can take the form

$$u = v + \lambda_1 g + \lambda_2 g\, y$$

The observed choices of *g* then maximize *u* subject to the valuation constraint

$$v = v(g, x)$$

However, note that whatever may be preference function of the board of directors or the management the actual value of *v* attained for a given *g* cannot exceed the value represented by the valuation frontier. Hence, a comparison of the ex ante valuation will be valid even in the more general context where the existence of adverse selection and moral hazard are acknowledged. The issue of identifying the control structure can be kept distinct from the estimation of the preference functions.

Notice that a given firm may adopt only one form of control or the other. Hence, it is generally not possible to estimate the valuation under both the control structures to set up a comparison. A practical approach, based on the decision making idiosyncracies under different forms of control, is necessary. This ex post approach has the following advantages:

(a) it provides the reasons for the specific strategic choices of the firm,

(b) the factors underlying the choice of the control structure can be exhibited, and
(c) the preference function and the extent of efficiency in decision making can be identified.

However, the presently available literature is inadequate

(a) in the choice of functional forms for the valuation frontier and preference function,
(b) in locating the sources from which the requisi e information can be extracted, and
(c) for defining efficient methods of estimation.

Most of the studies on corporate control consider

(a) the growth of the capital assets, and the capital structure decision as the fundamental long term strategic decisions, and
(b) wages and compensation policies as the important incentive, and the dividend payment as the essential constraint chosen by the board of directors in their effort to discipline the management.

An appropriate choice of the functional forms should therefore exhibit the ex post choices of these decisions as functions of the external market conditions (x) and the controls (y). That is, the choices resulting from the model specification should be of the form

$$g = g(x, y)$$
$$\theta = \theta(x, y)$$

where: g = growth of capital assets, and
θ = debt equity ratio

or a suitable variant depending on the locus of control.

The modelling exercise should also keep the following theoretical issues in perspective:

(a) the two major theoretical contributions covering the corporate control and capital structure decisions, viz., the Marris (1964) model and the bonding hypothesis of Grossman and Hart (1982) should be taken into account, and

(b) the channels through which incentives and constraints modify managerial behavior should be exhibited.

The problem of estimating the parameters of such a model could not be handled by conventional methods. Hence, there was a necessity to develop an appropriate procedure. Proper sources of information, which can be defended on the basis of economic theory, had to be identified to achieve identification of the parameters of the model. This study makes a theoretical contribution in both these directions.

8.2 The Theoretical Achievements

It was shown that the basic difference between the control structures with respect to decision making can be exhibited through a recursive model. In particular,

(a) the strategic choices in the governance mechanism depend on the market related variables and the government policies but not on the incentives and constraints, and

(b) the nature of the operation of the implicit contract is such that managerial decision making reflects their assessment of the market related variables as well as the constraints imposed by the board of directors.

By way of contrast the board of directors chooses incentives and constraints

(a) on the basis of the strategic choices in the case of governance mechanism to ensure their implementation, and

(b) purely on the basis of market constraints in the context of an implicit contract.

Both these alternatives are amenable to estimation due to their recursive structure.

The above model does not identify the reasons for the specific choices of the control structure. This had to be achieved through an alternative method. The salient steps of this procedure are:

(a) defining a set of variables which have a bearing on the market value of the firm,
(b) computing the principal component corresponding to the largest characteristic root, and
(c) defining the limits within which the choice of the implicit contract is more efficient.

This exercise had to be limited to a cross section sample of the firms due to certain methodological difficulties.

Whatever the locus of control the preferences in decision making can be modelled in the form

Maximize $U = V + C' \lambda Y$ (preference function)

Subject to $V = A_0 + C' A_1 C + C' A_2 X + A_3 Z$, *and*

Where, U = utility of the decision makers,
V = market value of the firm,
C = a (p*1) vector of decision variables,
X = a (q*1) vector of market related variables which have an effect on the choice of C,
Z = a (s*1) vector of market related variables and incentive and constraint variables which are expensive to adjust to, and
Y = a (r*1) vector of incentives and constraints

This specification has three specific properties:

(a) it sustains the specification of the choice of g and θ the form

$$g = g(X,Y)$$

$$\theta = \theta(X,Y)$$

(b) explicitly exhibits the weak bonding effects as the channel through which the Y variables affect strategic decisions, and

(c) incorporates the hypothesis of the Marris (1964) model and the strong bonding effects alluded to in Grossman and Hart (1982).

It was shown that the reduced form specification of C, viz.,

$$C = B_1 X + B_2 Y$$

Where $A_2 = -2 A_1 B_{1'}$,

$\lambda = -2 A_1 B_{2,}$ *and*

the reduced form specification of the expansion path represented by

$$V = A_0 + Y^{*\prime} A_1 Y^* - X^{*\prime} A_1 X^* + A_3 Z$$

Where $Y^* = B_2 Y$, *and*

$X^* = B_1 X$

provides all the necessary information to estimate the parameters of the model. If C is a scalar, e.g., only one decision is involved there is no identification problem. In the more general case the model is identifiable if and only if

$$p = \textit{minimum}\ (q, r).$$

8.3 The Empirical Results

The present study relates to the chemical industry of the corporate sector. It is based on the time series for 27 firms for which all the requisite data was available from the official directory of the Bombay stock exchange for at least 20 years between 1967 and 1994.

It was found that six firms had the governance mechanism in operation and the rest of the twenty one firms adopted the implicit contract as a control structure.

The following general features of the strategic choices emerged.

(a) The firms determine the growth of the capital assets on the basis of long run market opportunities rather than the short term market fluctuations. This can be inferred from the absence of business risk in most of the growth equations. The appearance of the financial risk in general indicates that they are sensitive to the cost factor while choosing the higher level of growth.

(b) In general, most of the firms follow the pecking order theory of corporate finance. That is, there is a general preference for internal sources to finance capital investments. However, when there are business opportunities which cannot be financed by the internal sources debt financing is restored to. For, the debt equity ratio increases with the market risk in several cases.

(c) In the context of the governance mechanism the choice of higher debt equity ratio and the associated costs induce the board of directors to offer better wages and salaries to the management to ensure bonding. The choice of dividend constraints is not influenced by these decisions.

(d) In the implicit contract framework the firms are

more sensitive to profit generation and the costs associated with the operating decisions in their choice of the capital structure. The incentives in the form of wages and salaries are provided to restrain the management from taking the financial risks inherent in the higher levels of debt equity ratio. However, dividend payments place a constraint on the choice of growth due to the managerial preference for internal financing of capital investments.

In sum, the information asymmetry and adverse selection implicit in the degree of business risk and the extent of control loss and moral hazard reflected by the financial risk have been found to decide the choice of the control mechanism. When the risks are low the board can make efficient decisions. When the risks are very high they prefer to regain control to keep the moral hazard in check. The implicit contract is the efficient control structure in all other cases.

The following conclusions emerge from the analysis of the preference model. For all the firms in the study the board of directors or the management has the choice with respect to one of the two strategic decisions alluded to above. They are averse to taking the risks of financing excessive growth by a high debt equity ratio. Four firms out of the six which have the governance mechanism as their control structure prefer growth as the major decision. In general, the board of directors takes into account the long term market opportunities in their choice of growth and the cost factor while choosing the debt equity ratio. In the case of firms for which the control structure is an implicit contract the management has a preference for growth in fifteen firms and the capital structure in the case of two firms. The other four firms did not exhibit any preference for either growth or capital structure. Instead the management is constrained to operate on the increasing portion of the valuation frontier.

In general, the management takes the product market conditions and internal sources of finances into account while choosing growth. They avoid the excessive debt equity ratio due to risk aversion. Consider those firms which exhibited a preference for growth. For many of these firms the debt equity ratio appears in the valuation frontier with a positive sign. This suggests the occurence of strong bonding effects in the sense of Grossman and Hart (1982). However, the variables representing incentives and constraints appear in the preference function more often. That is, the weak bonding effects are more prominent. Dividend constraints, instead of the wage payments, are more effective in achieving the weak bonding property.

The primary difference between these two control structures is their degree of relative risk aversion. The board of directors will resort to a governance mechanism only when they feel that the managerial decisions are the second best and/or the agency costs of achieving the efficient decisions are higher than the addition to the market value. There is no significant evidence of the management seeking or gaining corporate control.

8.4 Limitations

The approach of this study is subject to certain limitations in concepts and model specifications, inference procedures, and the data base. The following aspects should therefore be reexamined to make further progress.

(a) When the implicit contract is in operation the board of directors does not know the functions $g = g(X, Y)$ and $\theta = \theta(X,Y)$ which represent the strategic choices of the management. Instead, they can observe the g and θ choices. Hence, they base their choice of Y on the observed g and θ. The recursive model of the present study assumes that the adjustments in Y are instantaneous. Perhaps it would have been more realistic to take lagged values of g and θ in the choice of Y by the board of directors. However, this is not a serious limitation since no attempt was made to examine the preferences of the board in their choices of Y.

(b) It was noted in section 2.3.1 and 4.8 that there are difficulties in the classification of a given set of variables as C, X, or Y. In particular, it was acknowledged that some of the Y variables are decisions of the board of directors and hence endogenous to the system. A similar argument can be presented in the context of the government policy variables. Similarly, the market variables X themselves may be influenced by the choice of C. In other words, there are wide ranging interrelationship between C, X, and Y. The classification of these variables as either endogenous or exogenous is an analytical judgement based on the specific purpose for which the model is constructed.

(c) The more difficult problem is this. Just as a decision model was formulated for C a similar model reflecting the decisions of the board in their choice of Y could have been formulated. Simultaneous estimation of such models would be a formidable task. Y was eventually considered as exogenous while estimating managerial preferences.

(d) Assume that the management exhibits a preference for g. There can still be an upward shift in the valuation frontier indicating a strong bonding. This was sought to be captured by including θ and θ^2 as a Z variables. However, in section 4.2 it was pointed out that it can also be reflected by a positive sign on the $g\theta$ variable. Further experimentation is desirable.

(e) The inclusion of the short term working capital or

liquidity would apppear strange if the problem is designed in the usual market context. However, in the Indian context there are quantitative credit limits imposed by the banking system. It was necessary to treat the limits on working capital as a part of the environment in which the firms operate.

(f) The analysis of the reasons for the specific choices of control mechanism has been confined to the cross section sample alone. It has not been attempted for the time series method due to the methodological problems alluded to in the text.

(g) The empirical specification of the valuation frontier and the preference function can be at best approximate. It would be reasonable to include a random error term in the equation depicting the strategic choices. However, this may not strictly represent a decision error in the sense of Chow (1983). Hence, treating the estimate of B_1 and B_2 as stochastic and restructuring the test procedure using asymptotic normalities as in Rao (1965) would perhaps be justifiable.

(h) Observe that when the strategic decisions are represented by the reduced form, i.e., $C = B_1 X + B_2 Y$ they will have the form of Zellner's seemingly unrelated regressions. It may be useful to modify the estimation procedure accordingly.

(i) This model has implications for the agency cost literature. Since the ex ante valuation frontier was estimated it would have been possible to calculate the maximum possible market value. The difference between the maximum value and the realized value can be a measure of the agency cost. The problem, however, is that no control structure has been identified to achieve the maximum value. Similarly, it is not altogether clear whether the managerial or the institutional constraints are responsible for the reduction.

(j) Consider the policy implications of the study. Since the ultimate purpose is to devise incentives and constraints to attain the maximum possible market value it would be natural to investigate the reasons why the choices of Y by the board of directors is not optimal. From a conceptual viewpoint the choices of the management would coincide with the maximum value if and only if $\lambda y = 0$. For the maximum U is the same as maximum V irrespective of the choice of C. Since the specification of Y contains a constant

$$Y' = (1Y^{*\prime}), \text{ and}$$

$$\lambda = (\lambda_0 \lambda^*) \quad \text{so that}$$

$$\lambda Y = \lambda_0 + \lambda^* Y^* = 0 \quad \text{implies}$$

$$\lambda^* Y^* = - \lambda 0$$

which can be solved uniquely for Y^* if and only if $p = (r\text{-}1)$ and λ^* is non-singular. Hence, in general, it is difficult to ascertain the optimality of the Y chosen by the board. The policy issue needs a fresh appraisal.

(k) The incentives provided to the management would have been best reflected by the remuneration and perks paid to the management. However, such figures are not available on any consistent time series basis. The entire amount of wages and salaries was used as a proxy for the compensation and perquisites.

(l) Net fixed assets may be a better proxy for measuring the size instead of the net sales. However, it is difficult to make the choice on apriori theoretical grounds. In a related study on inventory decisions

Rao and Rastogi (1995) found net assets to be a better measure of size.

8.5 Extensions

The methodology of the present study has been able to provide a framework to examine managerial preferences. Further, it can be justified from both the theoretical as well as empirical points of view. It is therefore expected that it can be applied satisfactorily in a number of related problems. The following situations are illustrative.

(a) It should be expected that the control structure would be different in established industries like textiles or industries like electronics which have been experiencing rapid changes in technology. The governance mechanism could be in operation in such industries due to the high business risk and substantial capital investments.

(b) Throughout the 1980s and continuing into the 1990s there was an argument that the management attempted diversification strategies which are not commensurate with their competencies. This resulted in a wave of mergers and takeovers to refocus business activities in consonance with the core competencies of the firms. Was there an excessive diversification into noncore areas? Rao and Acharya (1995) reported some preliminary attempts to answer this question.

(c) The theoretical preference model has important implications for the short term decisions of the firm, viz., inventory, advertising and selling cost. Rao and Rastogi (1995) reported results for an inventory model. Similarly, work to investigate excessive advertising is in order. It would be even more important to extend these results to decentralized decision making within the firm.

(d) To introduce time lags into the model a preliminary decision must be made about their classification into the X and Y category. Irrespective of this decision the estimation problem involved in the use of lagged variables must be addressed while defining the reduced forms.

(e) The present study assumes that the firm utilizes the same control structure throughout the interval of time of the study. However, it should be possible to investigate the changes made over time if any. The switching regression method will be useful in such a context.

(f) Redefining the model in vector notation instead of the matrix notation utilized in the present study may facilitate examination of the identification problem in more general models as well.

On the whole, it can be claimed that this study offers a basic contribution to the area of corporate control and has the potential to extend it to several related areas.

References

Agrawal, A., and G.N. Mandelker (1987), Managerial Incentives and Corporate Investment and Financing Decisions, *Journal of Finance*, 42, 823-837.

Aoki, M. (1990), Towards an Economic Model of the Japanese Firm, *Journal of Economic Literature*, 28, 1-27.

Balakrishnan, S., and I. Fox (1993), Asset Specificity, Firm Heterogenity, and Capital Structure, *Strategic Management Journal*, 14, 3-16.

Balasubramaniam, N. (1993), *Corporate Financial Policies and Shareholders Returns: The Indian Experience*, (Bombay: Himalaya).

Barney, J.B. (1986), Review of Economic Behavior within Organizations, *Administrative Science Quarterly*, 31, 140-142.

Barton, S.L., and P. J. Gordon (1987), Corporate Strategy: Useful Perspective for the Study of Capital Structure, *Academy of Management Review*, 12, 67-75.

Baumol, W.J. (1959), *Business Behavior, Value and Growth*, (NewYork: Macmillan).

Baumol, W.J. (1967), *Business Behavior, Value and Growth*, Revised Edition, (NewYork: Harcourt, Brace and World).

Baumol, W.J., et al (1970), Earning Retention, New Capital and the Growth of the Firm, *Review of Economics and Statistics*, 52, 345-355.

Benston, G. (1985), The Self-Serving Management Hypothesis: Some Evidence, *Journal of Accounting and Economics*, 7, 67-84.

Berle, A. A., and G. C. Means (1932), *The Modern Corporation and Private Property* (New York: Macmillan).

Blazenko, G. W. (1987), Managerial Preference, Asymmetric Information and Financial Structure, *Journal of Finance*, 42, 839-862.

Bolten, P., and J. Farrell (1990), Decentralization, Duplication, and Delay, *Journal of Political Economy*, 98, 803-820.

Bothwell, J. L. (1990), Profitability, Risk and the Seperation of Ownership from Control, *Journal of Industrial Economics*, 28, 303-312.

Brealey, R., and S. Myers (1984), *Principles of Corporate Finance*, (New York: McGraw-Hill).

Brickley, J. A., and C. M. James (1987), The Takeover Market, Corporate Board Composition and Ownership Structures: The Case of Banking, *Journal of Financial Economics*, 30, 161-180.

Cable, J. R. (1988), Organizational Form and Economic Performance, in S. Thompson and M. Wright (eds.), *Internal Organization, Efficiency and Profit*, (Oxford: Phillip Allen).

Carney, W. J. (1987), The Theory of the Firm: Investor Coordination Costs, Control Premiums and Capital Structure, *Washington University Law Quarterly*, 65, 1-67.

Chandler, A. D. (1977), *The Visible Hand: The Managerial Revolution in American Business*, (Cambridge: Harvard University Press).

Chang, S. J., and U. Choi (1988), Strategy, Structure and Performance of Korean Business Groups, *Journal of Industrial Economics*, 37, 141-158.

Chow, G. C. (1981), *Econometric Analysis by Control Methods*, (NewYork: Wiley).

Chow, G. C. (1983), *Econometrics*, (NewYork: Wiley).

Coase, R. L. (1937), The Nature of the Firm, *Economica*, 4, 386-405.

Conyon, J. M., and D. Leech (1994), Top Pay, Company Performance, and Corporate Governance, *Oxford Bulletin of Economics and Statistics*, 56, 229-247.

Conyon, J. M., P. Gregg, and S. Machin (1995), Taking Care of Business: Executive Compensation in the United Kingdom, *The Economic Journal*, 105, 704-714.

Copeland, T. E., and J. F. Weston (1988), *Financial Theory and Corporate Policy*, (MenloPark: Addison Wesley).

Cosh, A., and A. Hughes (1987), The Anatomy of Corporate Control: Directors, Shareholders and Executive Remuneration in Giant US and UK Corporations, *Cambridge Journal of Economics*, 11, 285-313.

Coughlan, A. T., and R. H. Schmidt (1985), Executive Compensation, Management Turnover, and Firm Performance: An Empirical Investigation, *Journal of Accounting and Economics*, 7, 43-66.

Cubbin, J., and D. Leech (1983), The Effect of Shareholding Dispersion on the Degree of Control in British Companies: Theory and Measurement, *Economic Journal*, 93, 351-369.

Cubbin, J., and D. Leech (1986), Growth Verses Profit Maximization: A Simultaneous Equations Approach to Testing the Marris Model, *Managerial and Decision Economics*, 7, 123-131.

Cyert, R. M. and J. G. March (1963), *A Behaviorial Theory of the Firm*, (Englewood Cliffs: Prentice-Hall).

DeAlessi, L., and R. P. Fishe (1987), Why Do Corporations Distribute Assets? An Analysis of Dividends and Capital Structure, *Journal of Institutional and Theoretical Economics*, 143, 34-51.

DeAngelo, H., and R. Masulis (1980), Optimal capital Structure Under Corporate and Personal Taxation, *Journal of Financial Economics*, 8, 3-29.

Demsetz, H. and K. Lehn (1985), The Structure of Corporate Ownership: causes and Consequences, *Journal of Political Economy*, 93, 1155-1177.

Dhrymes, P. J. (1970), *Econometrics*, (NewYork: Harper and Row).

Dixit, M. R. (1992), Monitoring the Government Policy Environment, in P. R. Shukla and S. K. Roychowdhry (eds.), *Private Sector and Economic Environment*, (New Delhi: Akashdeep).

Donaldson, G. (1961), Corporate Debt Capacity: A Study of Corporate Debt Policy and the Determination of Corporate Debt Capacity, *Boston: Division of Research, Harvard School of Business Administration.*

Drucker, P. F. (1986), *The Practice of Management*, (NewYork: Harper and Row).

Easterbrook, F. H. (1984), Two Agency Cost Explanations of Dividends, *American Economic Review*, 74, 650-660.

Eatwell, J. L. (1971), Growth, Profitability and size: The empirical Evidence, in R. Marris and A. wood (eds.), *The Corporate Economy*, (London: Macmillan).

Edwards, F. R. (1977), Managerial Objectives in Regulated Industries: Expense Preference Behavior in Banking, *Journal of Political Economy*, 85, 147-162.

Fama, E. F. (1990), Contract Costs and Financing Decisions, *Journal of Business*, 63, S71-S92.

Fama, E. F., and M. C. Jensen (1983), Seperation of Ownership and Control, *Journal of Law and Economics*, 26, 301-325.

Fazzari, S. M., and B. C. Peterson (1993), Working Capital and Fixed Investment: New Evidence on Financing Constraints, *Rand Journal of Economics*, 24, 328-342.

Ferri, M. G., and W. H. Jones (1979), Determinants of Financial Structure: A New Methodological Approach, *Journal of Finance*, 34, 1631-1644.

Fillipi, E., and G. Zanetti (1971), Exogenous and Endogenous Factors in the Growth of Firms, in R. Marris and A. Wood (eds.), *The Corporate Economy*, (Cambridge: Harvard University Press.)

Flath, D., and C. R. Knoeber (1985), Managerial Sharholding, *Journal of Industrial Economics*, 34, 93-100.

Francis, A. (1980), Company Objectives, Managerial Motivations and the Behavior of Large Firms: An Empirical Test of the Theory of Managerial Capitalism, *Cambridge Journal of Economics*, 4, 349-361.

Freind, I., and L. Lang (1988), An Empirical Test of the Impact of Managerial Self-Interest on Corporate Capital Structure, *Journal of Finance*, 43, 271-281.

Garen, J. E. (1994), Executive Compensation and Principal Agent Theory, *Journal of Political Economy*, 102, 1175-1199.

Garvey, G., and N. Gaston (1991), Delegation, the Role of Managerial Decisions as a Bonding Device and the Enforcement of Implicit Contracts, *Advances in Econometrics*, 9, 87-120.

Glazer, J., and R. Israel (1990), Managerial Incentives and Financial Signalling in Product Market Competition, *International Journal of Industrial organization*, 8, 271-280.

Gordon, R. A. (1961), *Business Leadership in the Large Corporation*, (Berkeley: University of California Press).

Grabowsky, H. G., and D. C. Mueller (1972), Managerial and Stockholder Welfare Models of Firm Expenditures, *Review of Economics and Statistics*, 54, 9-24.

Green, R. (1984), Investment Incentives, Debt and Warrents, *Journal of Financial Economics*, 13, 115-135.

Grossman, S. J., and M. H. Miller (1988), Liquidity and Market Structure, *Journal of Finance*, 43, 617-637.

Grossman,S. J., and O. D. Hart (1982), Corporate Financial Structure and Managerial Incentives, in J. J. McCall (ed.), *The Economics of Information and Uncertainty*, (Chicago: University Chicago Press).

Hambrick, C. D., and S. Finkelstein (1995), The Effects of Ownership Structure on Conditions at the Top: The Case of CEO Pay Raises, *Strategic Management Journal*, 16, 175-193.

Harris, M., and A. Raviv (1988), Corporate Control Contests and Capital Structure, *Journal of Financial Economics*, 20, 55-86.

Harris, M., and A. Raviv (1990), Capital Structure and the Informational Role of Debt, *Journal of Finance*, 45, 321-349.

Harris, M., and A. Raviv (1991), The Theory of Capital Structure, *Journal of Finance*, 46, 297-355.

Harris, M., and A. Raviv (1992), Financial Contracting Theory, in J. J. Laffont (ed.), *Advances in Economic Theory*, (Cambridge: Cambridge University Press).

Hart, O. (1995), Corporate Governance: Some Theory and Implications, *The Economic Journal*, 105, 678-689.

Hassid, J. (1977), Diversification and the Firm's Rate of Growth, *Manchester School of Economics and Social Studies*, 48, 16-28.

Heal, G. M., and A. Silberston (1972), Alternative Managerial Objectives: An Explanatory Note, *Oxford Economic Papers*, 24, 137-150.

Herendeen, J. B. (1975), *The Economic Theory of the Corporate Economy*, (NewYork: Dunellen).

Hexter, J. L. (1975), Entropy, Diversification, and the Information Loss Barrier to Entry, *Industrial Organization Review*, 3, 130-137.

Hill, C. W. L., and T. M. Jones (1992), Stakeholder Agency Theory, *Journal of Management Studies*, 29, 131-154.

Hitt, M. A., and R. D. Ireland (1986), Relationship Among Corporate Level Distinctive Competencies, Diversification Strategy, Corporate Structure and Performance, *Journal of Management Studies*, 23, 401-416.

Hoeneck, S. A. (1983), *Economic Behavior within Organizations*, (NewYork: Cambridge University Press).

Holstorm, B., and J. Tirole (1993), Market Liquidity and Market Performance Monitoring, *Journal of Political Economy*, 101, 678-709.

Hoskisson, R. E., and T. A. Turk (1990), Corporate Restructuring: Governance and Control Limits of the Internal Capital Market, *Academy of Management Review*, 15, 459-477.

Hughes Hallet, A. J., and A. P. Ancot (1982), Estimating Revealed Preferences in Models of Planning Behavior, in J. H. Paelink (ed.), *Qualitative and Quantitative Mathematical Economics*, (The Hague: Martinus Nijohoff).

Jacquemin, A. P., and H. W. DeJong (1977), *European Industrial Organization*, (London: Macmillan).

Jarrel, G. A., and A. B. Poulsen (1988), Dual Class Recapitalization as Antitakover Mechanisms: The Recent Evidence, *Journal of Financial Economics*, 20, 129-152.

Jensen, M. C. (1986), Agency Costs of Free Cash Flow, Corporate Finance, and Takeovers, *American Economic Review*, 76, 323-329.

Jensen, M. C. (1993), The Modern Industrial Revolution, Exit and the Failure of Internal Control Systems, *Journal of Finance*, 48, 831-880.

Jensen, M. C., and J. B. Warner (1988), The Distribution of Power Among Corporate Managers, Shareholders, and Directors, *Journal of Financial Economics*, 20, 3-24.

Jensen, M. C., and R. S. Ruback (1983), The Market for Corporate Control, *Journal of Financial Economics*, 11, 5-50.

Jensen, M. C., and W. H. Meckling (1976), Theory of the Firm: Managerial Behavior, Agency Costs and Ownership Structure, *Journal of Financial Economics*, 3, 305-360.

Jorgensen, S., P. M. Kort, and G. C. V. Schijndel (1989), Optimal Investment Financing, and Dividends, *Journal of Economic Dynamics and Control*, 13, 339-377.

Kamecke, U. (1993), The Role of Competition for an X-Inefficiently Organized Firm, *International Journal of Industrial Organization*, 11, 391-405.

Kay, J. A. (1991), Economics and Business, *Economic Journal*, 101, 57-63.

Kay, J. A. (1995), *Foundations of Corporate Success*, (Oxford: Oxford University Press).

Kaysen, C. (1959), The Corporation: How Much Power?, What Scope?, in E. S. Mason (ed.), *The Corporation in Modern Society*, (Cambridge, Massachusetts: Harvard University Press).

Kim, W. S., and E.H. Sorensen (1986), Evidence of the Impact of the Agency costs of Debt on Corporate Debt Policy, *Journal of Financial and Quantitative Analysis*, 21, 131-144.

Kishore, B. (1981), *Corporate Capitalization in India*, (Bombay: Himalaya).

Klein, B., and K. B. Leffler (1981), The Role of Market Forces in Assuring Contractual Performance, *Journal of Political Economy*, 89, 615-641.

Kort, P. M. (1990), Dynamic Firm Behavior within an Uncertain Environment, *European Journal of Operational Research*, 47, 371-386.

Koutsoyiannis, A. (1978), Managerial Job Security and Capital Structure of Firms, *Manchester School of Economics and Social Studies*, 46, 51-75.

Koutsoyiannis, A. (1987), *Non-Price Decisions*, (Basingstone: Macmillan).

Krishnamurty, K., and D. U. Sastry (1975), *Investment and Financing in the Corporate Sector*, (Bombay: Tata McGraw Hill).

Kumar, N. (1984), Public Policy, Marris Model and Corporate Growth in India, *Indian Economic Journal*, 32, 74-83.

Larner, R. J. (1966), Ownership and Control in the 200 Largest Nonfinancial Corporations from 1929 to 1963, *American Economic Review*, 56, 777-787.

Leech, D., and J. Leahy (1991), Ownership Structure, Control Type Classifications and Performance of Large British Companies, *Economic Journal*, 101, 1418-1437.

Leibenstein, H. (1980), *Beyond Economic Man*, (Cambridge: Harvard University Press).

Lewellen, W. G., and B. Huntsman (1970), Managerial Pay and Corporate Performance, *American Economic Review*, 60, 710-720.

Lintner, J. (1956), Distribution of Income of Corporations Among Dividends, Retained Earnings, and Taxes, *American Economic Review*, 46, 97-124.

Lintner, J. (1971), Optimal and Maximal Corporate Growth Under Uncertainty, in R. Marris and A. Wood (eds.),

The Corporate Economy, (Cambridge: Harvard University Press).

Lyles, M. A., and C. R. Schwenk (1992), Top Management, Strategy and Organizational Knowledge Structures, *Journal of Management Studies*, 29, 155-174.

Magnus, J. R., and H. Neudecker (1988), *Matrix Differential Calculus*, (NewYork: Wiley).

Marby, B. D., and D. L. Siders (1967), An Empirical Test of the Sales Maximization Hypothesis, *Southern Economic Journal*, 3, 367-377.

Marris, R. (1964), *The Economic Theory of 'Managerial' Capitalism*, (NewYork: The Free Press).

Marris, R. (1971a), An Introduction to Theories of Corporate Growth, in R. Marris and A. Wood (eds.), *The Corporate Economy*, (London: Macmillan).

Marris, R. (1971b), The Modern Corporation and Economic Theory, in R. Marris and A. Wood (eds.), *The Corporate Economy*, (London: Macmillan).

Marris, R. (1971c), Some New Results on Growth and Profitability, in R. Marris and A. Wood (eds.) *The Corporate Economy*, (London: Macmillan).

Marsh, p. (1982), The Choice Between Equity and Debt: An Empirical Study, *Journal of Finance*, 37, 121-144.

McGuire, J. W., J. S. Y. Chin, and A. O. Elbring (1962), Executive Incomes, Sales and Profits, *American Economic Review*, 52, 753-761.

McInnes, J. M., and W. J. Carlton (1982), Theory, Models and Implementations in Financial Management, *Management Sciences*, 957-978.

Mehran, H. (1995), Executive Compensation Structure, Ownership and Firm Performance, *Journal of Financial Economics*, 38, 163-184.

Mester, L. J. (1989), Testing for Expense Preference Behavior: Mutual Versus Savings and Loan, *Rand Journal of Economics*, 20, 483-498.

Milgrom, P., and J. Roberts (1992), *Economics, Organization, and Management*, (Englewood Cliffs: Prentice-Hall).

Misra, G. D. (1984), *Investment, Financing and Earning in the Corporate Sector in India*, (Allahabad: Kitab Mahal).

Monsen, R. J., and A. Downs (1965), A Theory of Large Managerial Firms, *Journal of Political Economy*, 73, 221-236.

Morck, R., A. Schleifer, and R. W. Vishny (1988), Management Ownership and Market Valuation: An Empirical Analysis, *Journal of Financial Economics*, 20, 293-315.

Mueller, D. C. (1967), An Experiment in the Measurement of Business Motivation, *Review of Economics and Statistics*, 49, 304-318.

Mueller, D. C. (1986), *Profits in the Long Run*, (Cambridge: Cambridge University Press).

Myers. S. (1984), The Capital structure Puzzle, *Journal of Finance*, 39, 575-592.

Myers, S., and N. Majluf (1984), Corporate Financing and Investment Decisions When Firms Have Information Investors Do Not Have, *Journal of Financial Economics*, 13, 187-221.

Nyman, S., and A. Silberston (1978), The Ownership and Control of Industry, *Oxford Economic Papers*, 30, 74-101.

Odagiri, H. (1981), *The Theory of Growth in a Corporate Economy*, (Cambridge: Cambridge University Press).

Ofek, E. (1993), Capital Structure and Firm Response to Poor Performance: An Empirical Analysis, *Journal of Financial Economics*, 34, 3-30.

Oliner, S. D., and G. D. Rudebusch (1992), Sources of Financing Hierarchy for Business Investment, *Review of Economics and Statistics*, 94, 643-654.

Palmer, J. P. (1973), The Profits Performance Effects of the Seperation of Ownership from Control in Large U. S. Industrial Corporations, *Bell Journal of Economics and Management Sciences*, 4, 293-303.

Radice, H. K. (1971), Control Type, Profitability and Growth in Large Firms, *Economic Journal*, 81, 547-562.

Rao, C. R. (1965), *Linear Statistical Inference and Its Applications*, (NewYork: Wiley).

Rao, T. V. S. R. (1988a), Demand Uncertainty, Decision Models of the Firm and Parameter Estimation, *Journal of Quantitative Economics*, 4, 45-58.

Rao, T. V. S. R. (1988b), Econometric Estimation of Decision Models Under Uncertainty, in J. K. Sengupta and G. K. KadeKodi (eds.), *Econometrics of Planning and Efficiency*, (Dordrecht: Kluwer Academic Publishers).

Rao, T. V. S. R. (1989), *Economic Efficiency of the Organizational Decisions of the firm*, (Heidelberg: Springer Verlag).

Rao, T. V. S. R. (1991), NIEO: Some Often Neglected Aspects of Specification and Inference, *Arthavijnana*, 33, 159-174.

Rao, T. V. S. R. (1994), Estimating Attitudes Towards Risk in a Volatile Environment, *Indian Journal of Applied Economics*, 3, 253-270.

Rao, T. V. S. R., and R. Rastogi (1995), Managerial Preference for Holding Inventory, *Indian Journal of Applied Economics*, 4, 27-53.

Rao, T. V. S. R., R. Rastogi, and S. Saha (1995), Capital Structure Decision: Implicit Contract or a Governance Relation? *International Review of Economics and Business*, 42, 145-162.

Rao, T. V. S. R., and R. Sharma (1984), Primacy of Corporate Dividend Decisions, *Indian Economic Journal*, 32, 56-72.

Rao, T. V. S. R., and S. Acharya (1995), Product Diversification and the Market value of the Firm,*Manuscript*.

Rao, T. V. S. R., and S. P. Singh (1987), Demand Uncertainty, Price Fixing Firms, and Parameter Estimation, *Economics Letters*, 24, 243-247.

Rao, T. V. S. R., and S. P. Singh (1990a), Core Vs. MLE for Decision Models Under Uncertainty, *Zeitschrift Fur Nationalokonomie*, 51, 145-158.

Rao, T. V. S. R., and S. P. singh (1990b), Core: For Decision Models Under Uncertainty, *Economics Letters*, 34, 43-48.

Rao, T. V. S. R., S. P. Singh, and P. P. Talwar (1991a), Estimation and Structure of Price-cost Margins Under Uncertainty, *Advances in Econometrics*, 9, 61-85.

Rao, T. V. S. R., S. P. Singh, and P. P. Talwar (1991b), Decisions of the Firm Under Uncertainty: Estimation and Structure of Price-Cost Margin, *International Review of Economic and Business*, 38, 355-368.

Rao, T. V. S. R., and S. Saha (1994), Interactive Effects of Organizational Structure and Control on Corporate Performance, *Journal of Quantitative Economics*, 10, 293-308.

Rediker, K. J., and A. Seth (1995), Board of Directors and Substitution Effects of Alternative Governance Mechanisms, *Strategic Management Journal*, 16, 85-99.

Rothenberg, T. J. (1971), Identification in Parametric Models, *Econometrica*, 9, 61-85.

Rozeff, M. S. (1982), Growth, Beta, and Agency Costs as Determinants of Dividend Payout Ratios, *Journal of Financial Research*, 5, 249-259.

Schleifer, A., and R. W. Vishney (1986), Large Sharholders and Corporate Control, *Journal of Political Economy*, 94, 293-309.

Schmalensee, R. (1988), Industrial Economics: An Overview, *Economic Journal*, 98, 643-681.

Schmalensee, R. (1989), Inter-Industry Studies of Structure and Performance, in R. Schmalensee and R. D. Willing (eds.), *Handbook of Industrial Organization*, (Amsterdam: Elsevier Science Publishers).

Sharma, R. (1986), *Corporate Financial Policy and Dividend Decisions*, (New Delhi: Deep and Deep).

Singh, A., and G. Whittington (1968), *Growth, Profitability and Valuation*, (Cambridge: Cambridge University Press).

Skilvas, S. D. (1987), The Strategic Choice of Managerial Incentives, *Rand Journal of Economics*, 18, 452-458.

Smith, C., and J. Warner (1979), On Financial Contracting: An Analysis of Bond Covennants, *Journal of Financial Economics*, 7,117-161.

Smith, C. W., and R. L. Watts (1992), The Investment Opportunity Set and Corporate Financing, Dividends, and Compensation Policies, *Journal of Financial Economics*, 32, 263-292.

Stephen, F., and S. Thompson (1988), Internal Organization and Investment, in S. Thompson and M. Wright (eds.), *Internal Organization, Efficiency and Profit*, (Oxford: Phillip Allen).

Stultz, R. M. (1988), Managerial Control of Voting Rights, *Journal of Financial Economics*, 20, 25-54.

Stultz, R. M. (1990), Managerial Discretion and Optimal Financing Policies, *Journal of Financial Economics*, 26, 3-28.

Taub, A. (1975), The Determinants of the Firm Capital Structure, *Review of Economics and Statistics*, 57, 410-416.

Teece, D. J. (1980), Economies of Scope and the Scope of the Enterprise, *Journal of Economic Behavior and Organization*, 1, 223-247.

Thompson, S. (1988), Agency Costs of Internal Organization, in S.Thompson and M. wright (eds.), *Internal Organization, Efficiency and Profit*, (Oxford: Phillip Allen).

Titman, S., and R. Wessels (1988), The Determinants of Capital Choice, *Journal of Finance*, 33, 1-19.

Turnovsky, S. J. (1970), Financial structure and the Theory of Production, *Journal of Finance*, 25, 1061-1080.

Vickers, D. (1968), *The Theory of the Firm: Production, Capital, and Finance*, (NewYork: McGraw-Hill).

Vickers, D. (1987), *Money Capital in the Theory of the Firm*,(Cambridge: Cambridge University Press).

Walter, J. E. (1963), Dividend Policy: Its Influence on the Value of the Enterprise, *Journal of Finance*, 18, 280-291.

Watts, R. L., and J. L. Zimmerman (1983), Agency Problems, Auditing, and the Theory of the Firm: Some Evidence, *Journal of Law and Economics*, 26, 613-633.

Whittington, R. (1988), Structure and Theories of Strategic Choices, *Journal of Management Studies*, 25, 521-536.

Williams, J. (1987), Perquisites, Risk and Capital Structure, *Journal Of Finance*, 42, 29-48.

Williamson, O. E. (1964), *The Economics of Discretionary Behavior: Managerial Objectives in a Theory of the Firm*, (NewYork: Prentice-Hall).

Williamson, O. E. (1971), Managerial Discretion, Organization Form and the Multi-division Hypothesis, in R. Marris and A. Wood (eds.), *The Corporate Economy*, (London: Macmillan).

Williamson,O.E. (1983), Organization Form, Residual Claimants and Corporate Control, *Journal of Law and Economics*, 26, 351-366.

Williamson,O.E. (1988), Corporate Finance and Corporate Governance, *Journal of Finance*, 43, 567-591.

Yarrow, G. K. (1973), Managerial Utility Maximization Under Uncertainty, *Economica*, 40, 155-173.

Yarrow, G. K. (1976), On the Prediction of Managerial Theories of the Firm, *Journal of Industrial Economics*, 24, 267-279.

Appendices

APPENDIX A

LIST OF THE FIRMS

Recall from chapter 5 that the study is based on 27 firms of the chemical industry. This appendix contains the names of the firms, arranged in the alphbetical order and their labels.

S. No.	*Name of the firm*	*Label*
1.	Albright Morarji Pandit Ltd.	Alb
2.	Alembic Chemicals Works Co. Ltd.	Alem
3.	Arlabs Ltd.	Arl
4.	BASF India Ltd.	BASF
5.	Bayer (India) Ltd.	Bayer
6.	Boots Pharmaceuticals Ltd.	Boots
7.	Borax Morarji Ltd.	Borax
8.	Cochin Refineries Ltd.	Coch
9.	Colour Chem Ltd.	Color
10.	Coromandel Fertilizers Ltd.	Coro
11.	DCW Ltd.	DCW
12.	Dharamsi Morarji Chemical Co. Ltd.	Dhm
13.	Glaxo Ltd.	Glaxo
14.	Gujarat State Fertilizers Co. Ltd.	Guj

15.	Herdillia Chemicals Ltd.	Herd
16.	IDL Chemicals Ltd.	IDL
17.	Indian Dyestuff Industries Ltd.	Dyes
18.	J. L. Morison (India) Ltd.	JLM
19.	Kanoria Chemicals Industries Ltd.	Kanor
20.	National Organic Chemical Industries Ltd.	NOCIL
21.	Polyolefins Industries Ltd.	Poly
22.	Rallis India Ltd.	Ralli
23.	Sandoz (India) Ltd.	Sand
24.	Synthetics Chemicals Ltd.	Synth
25.	Tata Chemicals Ltd.	Tata
26.	Unichem Laboratories Ltd.	Unic
27.	Union Carbide India Ltd.	Union

APPENDIX B

EXPLANATORY NOTES

The explanatory notes of the Bombay Stock Exchange official directory provide the information about the costruction of items and interpretation of the data of a company under the following heads:

(a) Comparative financial statements,
(b) Common-size financial statements,
(c) Trend Percentage,
(d) Ratio of items selected from the balance sheet and the profit and loss statements and from both the statements taken together,
(e) Equity data,
(f) Graphs and charts of equity prices, net sales, pre-tax profit, equity dividend, etc..

The definitions provided therein are reproduced verbatim.

(a) Book value per share shows the investment per share made in the business by the shareholders. In other words, it represents on a per share basis the net assets (excluding intangibles) remaining after offsetting all the liabilities against the assets. It is retention of profits after deducting the losses. It can be defined as

$$B = A + (R - I - D)/(E)$$

where B = book value per share, A = amount called up per share, R = shareholders' reserves, I = intangible assets, D = preference dividends in arrears, and E = no. of equity shares subscribed.

(b) The market price to book value ratio represents the market evaluation of every rupee of equity of the company and indicates the extent to which the market value of the equity is protected by the assets of the company taken at their book value. The ratio follows

$$M = AP/B$$

where M = market price to book value, AP = Average market price of the month in which the company's financial year ends, and B = book value per share.

(c) Net sales is derived by deducting goods returned, allowances and discount from the gross amount received from sales. It indicates the soundness of the company.

(d) The net profit is arrived at by deducting the provision for taxes from the pre-tax profit.

(e) Inventory comprises goods held for sale or in the process of manufacture and supplies used up in operating the business. In the case of manufacturing companies, the item is subdivided into raw materials, semifinished, and finished goods.

(f) Interest includes interest paid on debentures and bonds and also on borrowed funds.

(g) The liquidity ratio, commonly referred to as the current ratio, provides a test of solvency and determines the short term financial strength. A ratio of two to one is considered satisfactory for industrial companies. It means that even if the value of the current assets were to shrink to one half, the creditors would receive payment in full. Some very successful companies operate efficiently on a current ratio of only one to one. A high ratio does not necessarily imply better liquidity. It is necessary to consider it in conjunction with the varying quality and charecteristics of the current assets.

Liquidity ratio = Current assets / Current liabilities

(h) It is clear from the profit and loss statement that the pre-tax profit is arrived at by adding or deducting the non-operating surplus or deficit as the case may be from the operating profit.

(i) Provisions for taxation provides an indirect check on the reported earnings. Weak companies tend to understate their tax liabilities, whereas at times an excess provision is made by some companies which do not desire to disclose to their shareholders the larger profits they may have earned. The tax provision in the profit and loss statement should be compared with the tax payable as calculated at the prescribed rates on the earnings reported in the statement. In many cases, there would be a significant variation between the two. The difference may be due to special provisions in the tax statutes, such as lower tax rates applicable to the initial slabs, or tax free interest income from gilt-edged investment, or less tax payable on intercorporate dividends, or carry forward of losses, or accelerated depreciation allowed for developmental purposes to specific industries etc..

(j) Capacity utilization, defined in the stock exchange official directory under the turnover ratio, is as follows:

Capacity utilization = Net sales / Total assets

where totat assets includes current assets, fixed assets and intangible assets.

(k) The cost of goods sold contains stock consumed, wages and salaries,and direct manufacturing expenses.

(l) Dividends per share shows the actual amount of dividend (gross) declared per share.

APPENDIX C

THE HISTORY OF THE FIRMS

C.1 A Preamble

In business decision making the theoretical arguments are always supplemented by certain practical considerations. Taking these aspects into account is crucial for testing the theoretical hypothesis as well as understanding and interprating the results obtained. It was therefore necessary to extract certain historical facts about each firm. To maintain the logical flow of the theoretical modelling these have been organized in the following sequence:

(a) incorporation and product lines,
(b) share prices and the market value of the firm,
(c) long term decisions,
(d) market related variables,
(e) incentives and constraints.

A brief history of each of the firm follows:

C.2 The Historic Profiles

C.2.1 Albright Morarji & Pandit Ltd.

The company was incorporated in 1965 as a result of the collaboration between Albright and Wilson Ltd., the Dharamsi Mororji Chemicals Ltd., and S.P. Pandit. The company manufactures phosphoric acid, sodium tripolyphosphate, sodium hexametaphosphate, and various other phosphorous products.

At the begining of the 1980s the company faced a recession, and a substantial reduction in profits. This resulted in some reduction in the share prices. However, the firm maintained its growth plan and financial investments through borrowings. In the late 1980s the firm started performing well. Sales and profits exhibited an upward trend.

The company undertook an expansion and modernization program in the following directions. (a) The company expanded the capacity of the sodium tripolyphosphate plant from 12 thousand tons to 25 thousand tons per year. (b) Set up a sulphuric acid plant and a sodium hexametaphosphate plant. They started manufacturing 14 thousand tons of linear alkyl benzene, 5 million square meters of gypsum, and 5 thousand tons of sodium tripolyphos per year. (c) The company entered into a joint venture with Albright Metal Finishing private Ltd. for manufacturing metal finishing chemicals.

Throughout the 1960s and 1970s the company experienced (a) sluggish demand for its products, (b) import of competing products by other agencies, (c) a rise in the prices of the principal raw materials, (d) labor problems and strikes, and (e) an increase in the wage bill.

For most of the time period under study the firm could only offer moderate levels of dividend. Given the market uncertainties it appears that the expansion policy would not have materialized if an implicit contract was in operation. A governance mechanism is more likely.

C.2.2 Alembic Chemical Works Co. Ltd.

The company was started in 1907 at Baroda. It produces chemicals, pharmaceuticals, pencillin, antibiotics, sulphuric acid, superphosphate, and other fertilizers. It also has Alembic Glass Industries Ltd. and other wholly owned subsidiaries.

For much of the time period under study there was an increase in the market value of the firm. Dividend payments were moderate and a preference for internal financing of investments is evident.

The growth of the firm was along the following lines. (a)The company increased the capacity of pencillin, streptomycin, erythromycin, antiinflamatory analgesics, and anti TB drugs. (b) With a view to achieve product diversification the company entered the area of veterinary and animal health care products like feed supplements, and antibiotics. (c) The neomer division of the company developed adequate capacity (to exploit economies of scale) of polypropylene, staple fibre, multifilament yarn, and other synthetic yarn.

Though sales increased over the years profit margins were eroded due to the following reasons: (a) The selling prices of most of the products remained stagnant due to the drug price control order. (b) Nonavailabilty of raw materials and an increase in the price of raw materials affected the costs of production adversely. (c) Periodic strikes by the employees resulted in a loss of large amounts of materials in the pipelines.

On the whole, there has been a moderate amount of consolidation by exploiting the existing distinctive competencies of the firm.

C.2.3 Arlabs Ltd.

Associated Research Laboratories was established in 1940 as a private limited company. It was incorporated as a public limited company in 1962. The company manufactures indigenous and synthetic dyestuffs, pigments, colors, chemical intermediates and so on.

For much of the time period under study the firm experienced a steady increase in sales and the market value of the firm. However, the profit position was never comfortable. Investments had to be financed mostly by borrowings.

Throughout the 1970s and the 1980s the firm experienced shortage of raw materials (particularly the imported inputs). To reduce some of the adverse effects of input availability the firm undertook backward vertical integration, appropriate diversification, and modernisation. In particular, the company started manufacturing disperse dyes, intermediates, and chemicals utilized mainly in the production of vat dyes.

The firm could not achieve the expected production levels and profit due to the following reasons. (a) There were interruptions in imported raw material. In particular, when the U.S.S.R. dishonoured a contract for raw materials worth Rs. 7.84 crores the company had to import costly raw materials from elsewhere. (b) Cost increases were mainly due to the devaluation of the rupee and increase in import duties. (c) There was a persistent shortage of working capital.

On the whole, it appears that the crucial diversification decisions could not be left entirely to the management. The board had to take control and decision making in its hands.

C.2.4 BASF India Ltd.

The company was started as a private limted company in 1943 and was converted into a public limited company in 1967. The primary products of the firm are styropor (expandable polystyrene), thermocole (expanded polysterene), and basyntan (synthetic tannning agents).

During the 1970s and the 1980s some divisions, viz., inorganic chemicals agrochemicals, dyestuffs, and plastics, performed well. However, the markets for organic chemicals, leather chemicals, and thermocole remained stagnant. Limitedprofitability restricted the firm to expansion within the existing product lines mainly to consolidate its market share.

The profit margins did not rise in proportion to sales due to the following reasons: (a)There was a recession in the demand for polystyrene products and dyestuffs. (b) The leather division was set back due to the gulf war and sluggishness in the U.S.S.R. market demand. (c) There was a significant uncertainty in the availability of raw materials and a substantial increase in the cost of raw materials. (d)

Increase in import duties and the appreciation of the Deutsch mark added to the cost escalation. In general, the firm reacted to the changes in the market, made attempts to consolidate its market position, and until the 1990s did not find any avenues for a major expansion.

C.2.5 Bayer(India) Ltd.

Bayer (India) Ltd. was incorporated in 1958 as private limited company. It was converted to a public limited company in 1960. Rubber chemicals and intermediates, pharmaceuticals and health care products, and agrochemicals are the major lines of production.

The market value of the firm increased steadily over the time period of the study. The firm (a) kept the dividend payments at moderate levels, and (b) financed their expansion plans from the internal sources whenever possible. This resulted in a depressed stock price and forced Bayer to finance their major expansion by borrowing from the term lending institutions.

Almost throughout the time period under study both the rubber chemicals division and the pharmaceuticals division recorded a strong growth of domestic as well as export demand. Throughout the late 1960s and the 1970s there was (a) a significant expansion in the capital assets of these divisions, (b) diversification into various activities including backward vertical integration into the manufacture of raw materials like toulene di-isocynate, and (c) a continuous R and D effort for adapting products to Indian conditions. These efforts contributed to the increase in market share.

After 1985 Bayer (a) diversified into formulations, and (b) modernized the production processes of bulk drugs. This strategy of a more appropriate product mix, and better capacity utilization improved the profitability of the pharma division.

However, profits did not increase in proportion to sales.

The basic reasons were the following. (a) The bulk drug division was subject to the drug price control order. (b) Cost control was not effective due to unfavourable exchange rates of the Deutsch Mark and the Yen, and (c) labor union problems and loss of production exaggerated the irreducible overhead costs.

C.2.6 Boots Pharmaceuticals Ltd.

The company was started in 1964 as a private limited company. It was converted into a public limited company in 1965. The leading lines of manufacture include insulin injections, pencillin and vitamin preparations, anti-dysentry drugs, household remedies, the Mindif series of animal health care products, and agrochemicals.

During 1986 the Boots company of U.K. voluntarily decided to dilute its shareholding by disinvesting 3 lakh equity shares of Rs. 10 par value at a premium of Rs. 45 per share. These shares were offered to the resident equity shareholders as a right issue.

The company has been consistently experiencing a strong trend in sales, profits, and the market value of its assets. Branded pharmaceuticals made a major contribution to sales. Similarly, the exports to the fareast and the middle east improved its sales.

As a measure of expansion the company (a) started manufacturing some new products like ibuprofen, domepin, hydrochloride and its formulations, (b) undertook backward vertical integration, (c) emphasized capacity utilization, and (d) established new sales depots to strengthen the distribution arrangements.

At the operational level the firm sought to increase profits through planned changes in the product-mix, increases in capacity utilization, and rigid control on expenses in all the areas of the company's operations.

C.2.7 Borax Morarji Ltd.

Borax Morarji Limited, a joint venture promoted by the Dharamsi Morarji Chemical company and Borax Holding Ltd. of U.K. was incorporated in 1963. They manufacture borax, boric acid, their derivatives, byproducts, and compounds.

Throughout the 1960s and the 1970s the company experienced (a) periodic and uncertain fluctuations in the demand for its products and compounds, and (b) erratic raw material supply. This resulted in a lack luster performance and even the stock prices were generally depressed. This resulted in a pressure to pay dividends. They were maintained at about Rs. 10 per share.

During 1985 the firm experienced a change in its fortunes. The licensed capacity of boric acid was increased by 867 tons per year under the reendorsement of licensed capacity scheme. Since then the firm experienced (a) a steady increase in the demand for its products, and (b) a favourable upward trend in its share prices. This allowed the management to utilize the internally generated finances for capital expansion and turn the corner.

The profit position was almost always determined by (a) the demand for export of its products, and (b) the fluctuations in the exchange rates which had a major influence on the cost of raw material imports.

C.2.8 Cochin Refineries Ltd.

The refinery was started in 1963. At the the outset it was designed to handle 50 thousand barrels of crude oil per day. They had a technical service agreement with the Phillips Petroleum Company of Oklahome, U.S.A.. The Phillips Company divested its holding in 1988. It was initially financed by borrowing since the company had a difficulty in selling the shares. Eventually the Kerala State Industrial Development Corporation bought a major part of the shareholding of Phillips.

The market value of the firm showed a significant increase only after the major global price change in 1979. Even after 1979 a significant part of the change was due to capacity expansion.

There were significant capacity expansions throughout the period of existence of the firm. In particular, (a) the handling capacity was increased to 90 thousand barrels per day by 1991, (b) they constructed a fluid catalytic cracking unit in the 1980s to increase the yield of LPG and middle distillates, (c) the firm installed digital control systems in all the process units, (d) the company diversified into the production of benzene, toulene, and polybutanes, and (e) created wagon loading and pipeline facilities to improve distribution.

However, there were major safety problems and breakdowns on several occasions. They resulted in a loss of production. For several years in the sample capacity utilization was not a well planned reaction to market conditions. Instead it was mainly governed by these unforseen circumstances.

The none too comfortable profit position suggests that the choice of the debt equity ratio was subservient to the growth decision despite its cost implications.

C.2.9 Colour Chem Ltd.

Incorporated in 1956 color chemicals has technical collaboration with Bayer AG and Hoechst AG of Germany. They manufacture pigments, pigment emulsions, chemicals, dyes, and manures. During 1988-89 Bayer AG transferred its shareholding to Hoechst AG. However, the technical collaboration is maintained. The company did not experience any basic change due to this realignment.

Throughout the time period under study there was a steady increase in the market value of the firm. They maintained a fairly steady dividends per share to generate internal sources of finances for capital investments. Additional finances were generally raised from the Unit Trust of India and other term lending institutions. The long term strategic decisions of the firm can be summarized as follows. (a) There is an awareness of the need to upgrade technology continuously. (b) A strategy of product diversification, specially backward vertical integration into pigments was taken up. (c) Proper choice of product mix and improvement in operating efficiency were considered essential to maintain its market share. (d) Marketing synergies were also established through joint ventures in Sri Lanka and elsewhere.

The short run performance of the firm was affected by several factors. (a) The markets for its products, both domestic and international, have been quite good. However, there were market risks due to the competitive market in which they operate. (b) Since the firm is a producer of intermediate products the fortunes of downstream firms affected their sales. In particular, during the 1980s the textile strike in Bombay created a reduction in demand. Similar problems were recorded even in the case of paints and varnishes. (c) Shortage of specific raw materials added to the costs of production.

C.2.10 Coromandel Fertilizers Ltd.

The company was incorporated in 1961 as a private limited company and was converted into a public limited company in 1964. It was promoted by California Chemicals and the International Minerals and Chemicals Corporation of the U.S.A.. The company produces complex fertilizers and urea under the brand name Gomor.

The market value of the firm declined for some time when they had transportation problems and a reduction in sales. The position improved subsequently. The firm paid moderate but relatively steady dividends. The share prices did not increase significantly.

The long term strategies of the firm can be described as follows. (a) The company increased the capacity of its plants by 38 %. (b) Replacement of the heat exchanger, modifications in the compressor design, and modernization of the plant stabilized its operations. (c) To popularize the brand name and gain an experience of marketing and distribution techniques the firm imported ammonium phosphate and other complex fertilizers and marketed them with the help of EID Parry India Limited.

The firm confronted two major problems. (a) Since fertilizers are bulky products there is a high transportation cost and limits the market to a specific geographic area. (b) Natural disasters like cyclones in Andhra pradesh affected production as well as market demand. In general, the firm was more inclined to consolidate its market position rather than seek aggressive growth.

C.2.11 DCW Ltd.

Dhangadhra Chemical Works was incorporated in 1939 as a private limited company . It was converted into a public limited company in 1943. The major products of the firm are (a) soda ash and other salts, (b) chemicals and essence (c) cordials, acids, and alkalies, and (d) pharmaceuticals and drugs. These products are sold under the brand name Horse Shoe.

Dividend payments were not very regular and the stock prices was generally depressed. The company financed much of its investment by borrowings from the IFCI and other term lending institutions. However, the stock price improved after 1990. In May 1994 the company launched an Euro issue for 25 million U.S. dollars by way of global depository receipts to finance its expansion activities.

The long term decisions of the firm were as follows. (a) The initial expansion of the soda ash plant was completed in 1980. The next expansion was expected to be completed by the end of 1991. (b) During 1986-90 improvements in the R and D activities enabled the firm to achieve higher production of PVC resins. To overcome the uncertain supply and the hike in the international prices of vinyl chloride monomer the company erected a total storage capacity of 5,600 tons. Under the modernization plan the capacities of the PVC plant and the beneficiated ilemenite unit were increased to 40 thousands and 25 thousands tons per year respectively. (c) Some new products, viz., ammonium bicarbonate, bromine hexa chlorethene, calcium carbide, and magnesium chloride were introduced recently.

The short term production, sales, and profit were determined by the following factors. (a) Throughout the time period under the study the performance of both the soda ash and the caustic soda units was not completely satisfactory on account of the sluggishness in the demand and severe competition. (b) The other plants, viz., the liquid chloride plant and tri perchloroethylene unit recorded an upward trend in profits during 1975-85 though the demand for these products was not encouraging. (c) There were difficulties in procuring calcium carbide even at higher prices. (d) The beneficiate ilamenite plant was mostly dependent on the export markets.

C.2.12 Dharamsi Morarji Chemical Co. ltd.

The company was started in 1919 at Bombay. The basic product lines consist of acids, heavy chemicals, superphosphate fertilizers, and other allied products. The company's products are still under the brand name 'Ship'.

For much of the time period under study the dividend payments were fairly highand regular. This resulted in increase in the market value of the firm.

During 1960s and 1970s the company undertook major expansions in the following directions: (a) The company expanded the triple superphosphate plant and doubled the capacity of the chlorosulphonic acid unit. (b) The company launched new products, e.g., sodium silica fluroide, aluminium fluroide, sodium ammonia sulphate, paramino phenol, activated silica etc.. (c) The capacity of sulphuric acid plant and single superphosphate plant was increased. (d) With a view to further diversification the company took another company on lease for the manufacture of resorcinol, a chemical product used by the tyre industry.

Till 1980 the company experienced (a) uncertainties and erratic supply of raw materials, (b) decrease in exports and sales after devaluation and inadequate government assistence, (c) inadequate rainfall and unprecedented drought in the company's market zone, (d) a fall in the average price due to the competition, increase in manufacturing cost, depressed demand and underutilization of the production capacity of fertilizers, (e) large carryover of the stock which led to higher interest charges, and (f) shut down of the plants and heavy payment of demurrage due to congestation at the Bombay Dock.

Despite the above casualities the company's sales performance was good and always increasing. However, the profit margins were under pressure.

The company adopted a suitable marketing strategy to improve the conditions by offering its sulphuric acid plant on a turn key basis to other parties. It entered a contract for the supply of technical knowhow and environmental engineering design for the effluent treatment plants.

C.2.13 Glaxo Ltd.

The company was incorporated as a private limited company in 1924 and was converted into a public limited company. The company produces, distributes and sells pharmaceutical, medical, chemical, biological, immunological, contraceptive, theraputic preparations, foods for infants, valid dietetic foods, cereals and foodstuffs of all description, all classes and kinds of chemical cosmetics, and dairy farm and garden produce.

Till 1975 the company faced (a) the impact of inflation on wage cost and material prices at a time when selling price of the products were rigidly controlled by the government, (b) scarcity of raw materials, temporary shortage of milk and agricultural inputs, (c) the impact of devaluation on the prices of imported chemicals, and (d) a high level of development expenditure which the firm was undertaking during that period.

Due to the above reasons the profitability position was under pressure which affected the market value of the firm. However, after 1978 it showed a significant increase. The preference for internal financing resulted in a low debt equity ratio.

The company made progress in modernizing the plants by extending the facilities and diversifying to other product lines. The growth of the firm is along these lines. (a) Some new products, viz., new ointments and other food products were launched. (b) The government approved an expansion of 25 percent in the company's milk food production capacity and vitamins. (c) Forty five new laboratory chemicals were added. (d) A microbiological laboratory was set up for development work. (e) Eighty nine new chemicals were introduced including high purity electronic grade materials. (f) The company raised the infant milk food products to 4000 TPA. (g) New operation based research system was introduced.

The net sales of the company in every division continued to show a steady increase. The demand exceeded the supply. Intense efforts were made to improve production efficiency and general working condition. The profit position also improved further in the 1980s. Price revision by the government improved the market share. The cost escalations were neutralized through the rationalization and simplification of the management process. The company exported to the U.K., U.S.S.R., and other countries. The company paid dividends regularly but at a moderate level.

C.2.14 Gujarat State Fertilizers Co. Ltd.

The company was incorporated in 1962 and was sponsered by the government of Gujarat state. The company manufactures and deals in artificial fertilizers, heavy chemicals, cement, coke, and their byproducts.

The share prices were depressed during the 1970s due to the fluctuations in the production and decline in the profit position. The market value of the firm showed an increase only after 1980.

Distinctive competencies of the firm enabled it to achieve tremendous growth and expansion. The company set up a R and D department and this was expanded by the commission of a new biotechnology facility and the establishment of a modern industrial corrosion and materials laboratory. The company expanded (a) existing nitrogenous fertilizer facility by establishing an ammonia plant of 350 TPA and urea plant 1,600 TPA. (b) purage gas recovery plant, nylon 6 plant another sulphuric acid plant for the manufacturee of 1,32,000 TPA sulphuric acid, melamina project, nylon shipping unit, further ammonia plant, and steam and power plant, and (c)thirty two items were developed and procured indigenously effecting substantial savings in foriegn exchange.

The large scale expansion forced the company to borrow from the term lending institutions and from foreign financial institutions for its foreign exchange requirement. Some plants were made available to the company under a credit arrangement between Indian banks and Exim bank of Japan.

The company recorded a significant increase in production as well as sale. The capacity utilization was more than 100 percent and in some cases it crossed 150 percent.

The company faced the following problems: (a) power supply disturbance, unprecedented floods and droughts, (b) mechanical failure and plant closure, (c) steep rise in the prices on all fronts which resulted in consumer resistence and led to the accummulation of stock, (d) strike by officers and go slow by workers, and (e) cheaper imported caprolactum.

The company paid regular and high dividends.

C.2.15 Herdillia Chemicals Ltd.

The company was promoted by E.I.D. parry Limited, Madras in collaboration with the Distillers Company Limited and Hercules Power Company U.S.A.. The company produces heavy organic chemicals and their derivatives, by products, co-products, and compounds from petrochemical raw materials.

The market value of the firm was fluctuating throughout the study period. The firm paid fairly high dividends. Though the company preferred internal financing for growth it had to borrow from ICICI and other financial institutions and foreign financial institutions.

The company expanded in the following dimensions. (a) Two diesel generating sets were commissioned to meet the power demand. (b) The phenol plant was shut down for renovation and modernization. (c) An improved type of catalyst for the phthalic anhydride plant was commissioned. (d) Additional equipments were installed in most of the plants. (e) Plants for the recovery of cumene and fumaric acid from byproduct stream were commissioned. (f) The company developed phenol xylyl ethane (PEX) a fluid used in high tension capacitors and the government approved the manufacturing with a capacity of 2,000 TPA. (g) The alkyl phenols and two speciality chemicals were commissioned. The isophorone plant and debottlenecking of diacetone were expected to be commissioned by the end of 1993.

Throughout the study period the company experienced (a) erratic supply of raw materials and power, (b) availability of cheap and excessive imports which affected the sales and selling price, (c) inadequate facilities in the Bombay port to handle hazardous bulk chemicals, (d) fire accidents, torrential rain and flooding at the factory area, strike at the factory, (f) increase in energy cost, higher charges of interest cost due to borrowings and high wage bills, (g) rupee devaluation and pressure on profit margins.

Despite these problems the company tried its best to overcome and to maintain profit margins. However, it could not succeed fully. Sales showed an increase. Better production and control of cost could not fully reverse the steep fall in the profits. Though in the 1980s the profit improved, high costs salaries and borrowings reduced the margins again. The dividend payments were kept at a moderate level.

C.2.16 IDL Chemicals Ltd.

The company was started in 1961. The company's products are detonators, detonating type explosives, accessories, safety type blasting equipments, exploders, and other accessories and equipment required for blasting.

The regular dividend payments resulted in above normal share prices. The firm expanded its product line in the following directions: (a) It started manufacturing delay detonators by assembling imported filled shells with indigeous components and undertook the phased indigenous production of half second and millisecond delay detonators. (b) PETN explosive plants were started in Rourkela, Hyderabad, and Bhiwani. (c) The firm received licence for the manufacture of 500 exploders per annum for gassy mines in collaboration with a company of Austria. (d) It manufactured pharmaceutical products with the amalgamation of Mysore Industries Testing Laboratories but later it was transferred to Astra-IDL Limited and closed the business. (e) It expanded in the new business of explosive cladding, hot rolled cladded coils of stainless steel and hot rolled non-ferrous cladded material. (f) Bulk explosive, bitumen emulsions plants nwere set up. (g) With a motive to diversify in gypsum products for building material the company associated itself with Coromandel Gypsum Limited, (h) The R and D wing developed technology for sodium aziz, vanillin and for new types of processes in delay element manufacture.

Production and sales both showed an upward trend. The company experienced problems, e.g., labor trouble, accident in the plant and shortage of critical raw materials which resulted in the low profitability.

C.2.17 Indian Dyestuff Industries Ltd.

The company started in 1959 at Bombay. The company manufactures vat dyes, pigments, intermediates for dyes, agrochemicals, pharmaceuticals, paints, plastics, and optical whiteners.

Throughout the study period the low profitability caused depressed share price. This resulted in a pressure to pay dividend regularly. Insufficient internal funds forced the company to borrow money from the term lending institutions, viz., IDBI, ICICI, IFCI, LIC, IRBI, and SICOM.

The company undertook the growth of the capital assets in two phases in the following directions. The firm (a) increased the capacity of vat dyes from 625 TPA to 10,825 TPA and that of reactive dyes from 180 TPA tp 600 TPA, (b) received licence for manufacture of 3,000 TPA of hydrosulphite of soda and licence was revised to 10,250 TPA, (c) expanded the sulphuric acid capacity by 16,500 TPA to 33,000 TPA, (d) completed the phthalic anyhdride plant for the manufacture of 9,700 TPA, (e) started manufacturing of optical whitening agents and cyanuric chloride under industrial licence in 1986-87, (f) introduced a new range of dyes and chemicals with the help of R and D activities.

Despite the recessionary period in the world market during 1970s the company performed well and sales consistently increased. Profit margins were eroded due to the following reasons: (a) High cost of raw materials resulted in high overheads per unit of output at lower levels of production. (b) There was a slump in the textile industry, slackness in the demand and stiff competition from the small scale sector. (c) Wages and salaries went up .(d) There were severe restrictions on the imports of intermediates and steep hike in imported raw materials due to the devaluation of the rupee. (e) Drastic power cuts and labor strike caused frequent problems. (f) Inflationary pressure became a hinderance for growth in productivity and profitability. (g) Delayed realisation of sales revenues brought about a severe strain on the working capital resources and margins came under pressure.

The company had to raise the selling price of various products to neutralize the increased cost. The firm strengthened the export base through a marketing organization in London to cater to the European market.

C.2.18 J.L.Morison (India) Ltd.

The company was incorporated in 1934 at Bombay. The company manufactures and distributes fertilizers, pharmaceuticals, proprietary products and chemicals. It used 'Novutox', 'Xylotox', 'Optex', 'Morison', 'Feedrite', 'Dr.Whites' etc. as brand names.

The share prices increased after 1980. The firm undertook a very moderate level of expansion. Some new products were introduced by the company, viz., surgical sutures, nivea liquid, nivea fine talc, nivea dry skin lotion, dental aids, aftershave moisturiser, shaving cream, and tender care prickly heat powder. The company availed modernization loan from KSIDC. It had collaboration and agreement with different companies in the U.K. and the U.S.A. for the manufacturing and marketing of a wide range of health care products.

There was an erosion of profits due to rising costs. The following reasons can be cited: (a) Drug price control order disrupted normal selling. (b) Short supply of more profitable products, restricted and interrupted supply of power, and raw materials caused problems. (c) Sales declined due to the cessation of the sole distribution agreement with Beechan private limited and a revised arrangement for acting as a commission agent for the products of Smith and Nephew (India) limited. (d) Prolonged strike and laying off workers affected the production adversely. (e) Steep rise in material and labor cost. (f) Underutilization of production facilities and inefficient management of resources.

Substantial control over the material cost and optimum capacity utilization helped in reducing the losses. Exports were made to West Germany, Bangladesh, Mauritius, and Sri Lanka. However, the profits declined after 1985.

The name of the company was changed in 1987 from J.L. Morison, sons and Jones (India Limited) to J.L. Morison (India) Limited. The dividend payments were made at moderate levels and were irregular.

C.2.19 Kanoria Chemicals and Industries Ltd.

The company was started in 1960 at Calcutta with the main objectives of manufacturing heavy chemicals.

A high leverage ratio and low profitability resulted in a depressed share price and in turn, a low market value of the firm. The firm invested capital and diversified along these lines. (a) Set up a modern fusion plant to manufacture caustic soda, solid/flakes with a capacity of 33,000 TPA, and a plant to produce 5,000 TPA of stable bleaching powder and increased the capacity of 15,000 TPA. (b) The company commenced production of Benzene hexachloride with 16,000 TPA capacity. (c) It diversified in manufacturing of jute yarn webbing, ressians, sacking, cotton bagging and soil saver. In 1988 the company transferred the assets of the Indian branch of

Ludhlow Jute Company to Aekta Limited, a subsidiary to the company. (d) For further diversification the company started for the manufacture of pentaerthrytol/pure and nitration grades with an installed capacity of 1,200 TPA which increased to 3,000 TPA and its byproduct sodium formate with 660 TPA. (e) The company strengthened the divisions through backward and forward integration by adding new product lines. (f) A plant was commissioned for the manufacture of formaldehydes. Another plant of poly propylene and lindane were set up in U.P..

Though the sales showed an upward increase, full benefits could not be realized due to power cuts. The company exported items. Large scale investments forced the company to borrow from the market. As of 31st March, 1992 the company had a total sum of Rs. 25.64 crores long term loan from financial institutions.

C.2.20 National Organic Chemical Industries Ltd.

NOCIL was started in 1961 at Bombay. It produces various organic and inorganic chemicals.

At the begining of the 1980s it earned high profit which resulted in a high share price and increase in the market value of the firm. The company took loan under the product loan arrangement scheme and expanded its activity in the following directions: (a) It established a gas cracking facility for the production of ethylene and propylene and increased the capacity of propylene to 300,000 TPA. (b) The production of PVC resins was raised from 20,000 TPA to 80,000 TPA, and that of ethylehexanol from 10,000 TPA to 30,000 TPA. (c) The firm started production of monocrotophos and dichloreoethane, the feed stock for vinyl chloride by converting the waste hydrochloride acid stream. (d) It received sanction to produce hydroxyle terminated polybutadiene and 20,000 TPA of high yielding varieties hybrid seeds. (e) Some new products like foot and mouth disease vaccine for cattle, phoratic, a insecticide, and isoproturon were being marketed by the company.

During 1970s the sales of the company improved due to higher unit prices but later it increased substantially due to increase in the market demand. It achieved improved operational efficiency at various plant levels and exported PVC resins to West Asia. At the same time the company experienced difficulties in maintaining the production level. The reasons are (a) a slump in the textile and surface coating industries, (b) an undesirable supply of electricity and mechanical problems, (c) port storage and handling facilities, (d) excise levies on chloride and oxygen which increased the cost of basic raw materials, and (e) supply of PVC resins at the international price which was lower than domestic price due to competition in the international market, (f) revision of the price of PVC resins downward due to the modvat scheme.

Despite bad working conditions the foreign collaborators gave sympathetic consideration for the operational difficulties encountered by the company and granted some concessions in respect of the product loan and operating service charges. Though the company had various market difficulties it paid high dividends to the shareholders.

C.2.21 Polyolefins Industries Ltd.

Polyolefins Industries Limited was incorporated in 1964. It was promoted by National Organic Chemical Industries Limited in collaboration with Hoechest AG of West Germany.

For much of the time period under study it experienced an increase in the market value of the firm. The stock prices of the firm always showed an upward trend. After the 1970s the company paid dividends regularly and at fairly high level. This resulted in the company financing its growth plans from borrowings. The firm had Rs. 16 crores as outstanding loan against term loans from ICICI, IDBI, AND HDFC etc..

The company had a good demand for its products in the domestic market but it had strong competition in the international market. The business risk was fairly high. The company undertook product diversification to reduce this risk in the following manner: (a) It started backward vertical integration. (b) It expanded the capacity of the high density polythylene plant and the pipe for water supply. (c) The effluent disposal plant was started with a installed capacity of 30,000 TPA which was increased by 46,990 TPA later. (d) It commissioned a plant for the manufacture of utilities like nitrogen, steam, cooling water, and polypropylene etc.. (e) Some other projects were undertaken for the manufacture of EVIA, pre-vulcanising inhibitor, sodium MBT, chlorinated polyethelene etc.. (f) The R and D department developed new rubber chemicals, intermediates and sodium bisulphide, and diamino elisulphide as antipollution measures.

In the early phases the company experienced cost escalation due to (a) an increase in the cost of imported raw materials created by the floating of Deutsche Mark, (b) high profit duties, (c) inflationary pressure, and (d) a hike in the price of naptha.

The company increased the dividend payments in the late 1980s.

C.2.22 Rallis India Ltd.

The company was incorporated in 1948 at Calcutta. It manufactures and sells pharmaceuticals, fertilizer mixtures, pesticides, hydrosulphite of soda, electric fans, petrol engines, and garments. It trades in fertilizers, cotton tanning materials, piece goods textiles, crushed bones, and marine products. The company has distribution arrangements for single and compound fertilizers, electrical appliances, power sprayers, electric fans, stationary and portable machine tools, pharmaceuticals, chemicals, and household products. The company is a recognized export house.

For much of the time period under study the unfavourable profit position resulted in a reduction in share price. Only after 1985, when the company showed an upward trend in its profit position, the market value of the firm increased. A fairly high dividend payment suggests that there is no preference for internal financing. Hence, the company depended on external financing to maintain its growth plans and expansion schemes. The company had four divisons viz., agrochemicals, engineering, merchandizing, and pharmaceuticals.

The growth plans of the company were along these lines. (a) It diversified and expanded its activity in the area of agrochemicals, viz., pesticides, organophosphate, and that of Ayurvedic products. (b) The engineering division diversified into printed circuit motors, washing machines, etc.. (c) The R and D center of the agrochemical division set up a comprehensive toxicological laboratory at Bangalore. (d) Fully export oriented basic chemicals manufacturing facilities were in progress. (e) The company entered into real estate development business.

Overall, the market for the company was booming and the turnover was substantial. The agrochemicals division registered growth in the begining but suffered later. The operation of the merchant division continued to be hampered by financial constraints and market conditions. The engineering division had an occasional imbalance in the production and it was sold to HMP group of companies. The pharmaceutical division showed an increase in the sales. But the profit margins were under pressure throughout the study period due to (a) financial constraints, credit squeeze and high interest rate, (b) shortage of raw materials and occasional imbalances in the production, (c) incidence of higher taxation including surtax and inflationary pressure, (d) removal of subsidy to agricultural products and drug price control order, (e) erratic monsoon and drought, (f) labor unrest, and (g) accumulation of stock.

In the 1980s the profits were commensurate with the growth of sales due to better efficiency at the operational level and through its modernization program. The company exported pesticides, chemicals and garments.

C.2.23 Sandoz (India) Ltd.

The company was registered in India in 1956 under the name of Sandoz products Limited for the sale and distribution of Products manufactured by Sandoz Limited of Switzerland. The trading company obtained permission to establish a new undertaking for the manufacture of calcium salts, pharmaceutical specialities, leucophor, textile chemicals, dyestuffs, agrochemicals, and chemical preparations of all kinds.

The firm experienced an increase in the market value of the firm and sales for much of the time period under study. The pressure on the profit margins did not allow the company to pay high dividends. Throughout the study period the company experienced (a) recessionary conditions prevailing in the country during the 1970s, (b) an increase in the general price level and cost of materials and energy, (c) drug price control order, (d) credit restrictions, high interest rate and weakening of rupee against major foreign currencies, and (e) extra payments and bonus to employees.

Despite the above problems the company undertook an expansion and modernization program. In particular, (a) The company undertook seed and plantlet project. (b) It established a plant for the manufacture of the active ingredient of podophylum and other vegetable drugs and introduced a preventive drug for asthama. (c) The calcium plant was substantially upgraded and registered as an export house. (d) The upgradation of agrochemicals, Synthetic plants and drugs was executed. (e) It commissioned a modern multipurpose plant for the production of leather chemicals and intermediates for agrochemicals. (f) The pharmaceutical division received a letter of intent for the manufacture of some new drugs and their formulations.

To improve the profitability the company changed its strategy of production. Better product mix and capacity utilization improved the conditions. Continued price ceiling and the favourable market for certain product groups also reduced the loss. The R and D department developed the basic information pertaining to the formulation and manufacturing of certain product pesticides. But due to increase in the provision for taxation it did not show much improvement. Drop in export to USSR also adversely affected the business to the rupee trade area. To meet its working capital requirement the company issued non convertible debentures.

C.2.24 Synthetics and chemicals Ltd.

The company was incorporated in 1960 for the manufacture of synthetic rubber and lattices of butadiene-styrene type, styrene and butadiene, and the raw materials necessary for the synthetic rubber plant.

Low profitability caused the depressed share prices. Dividends were irregular and were paid at a moderate level in the begining but at a high rate in the late 1980s. This reflects the preference for external financing. The company borrowed money from term lending institutions and foreign financial institutions to invest in the growth of the capital assets of the firm.

The company undertook its expansion in the following directions: (a) diversified into a new grade of rubber to cater to the needs of consumer industries. (b) The company established the second Horton sphere of 780 tonns for storage of butadiene and installed a terminal at Kandla for storage and handling of imported butadiene. (c) It started a new nitrate plant, expanded the latex plant and BD catalyst plants, SBR facilities to 80,000 TPA which resulted in an enhancement of SBR production capacity of 4,100 TPA . (d) In order to save energy a 3 MV condensing turbo generator was installed. (e) An industrial licence for the manufacture of styrenated phenol for captive consumption, of Polystyrene and of 30 million liters of ethyl alcohol was received.

During the study period the company experienced (a) an acute shortage of alcohol and an irregular supply of benzene, (b) a reduction in the profits and enhancement in the cost of production due to three fold increase in the price for imported alcohol, (c) accumulation of stocks and sluggish demand, (d) strike by workmen which necessitated some layoff, (e) low sale price for synthetic rubber applied by the government and excise duty on synthetic rubber.

In general, the sales and profits of the company had shown a downward tendency till 1975. After that period the production and sales went up but profits were still fluctuating.

C.2.25 Tata Chemicals Ltd.

Tata chemicals was incorporated in 1939 at Bombay. The firm manufactures salt, byproducts of salt alkalies, heavy chemicals and insecticides, and the technical and battery grades.

In general, the company showed a substantial increase in the market value of the firm. After 1980s the company performed well and profits also increased. This led the company to pay high dividends. A high payout ratio shows a preference for external financing. The major expansion and modernization program were the following: (a) It increased the capacity of sodium bicarbonate, hydrochloric acid, benzene, soda ash by 5,00,000 TPA, and of bromine by 475 TPA. (b) The firm modernized and rehabilated the existing facilities. (c) It set up a hydrogeneration plant to utilize the surplus generation from its caustic soda plant. (d) It started production of high quality iodised salt and phosphateic fertilizers. (e) It installed a modern circo fluid high pressure boiler capable of generating 900 tons of stream per hour at 110 kg/k m^2 and at 560 degree temperature. Low pressure turbo generators were also commissioned. (f) The DGTD registration was received for the manufacture of 15,000 TPA of unadulterated and environmentally safe detergent material. (g) The cement plant was expected to be commissioned in september 1993. (h) Equipments were added in a phased manner.

The sales of the company increased tremendously in one or two years. Though the sales were higher, the gains were eroded due to the following reasons: (a) It experienced an increase in sales tax rates and in the excise duty on furnace oil. The price of the coke, and gunny bags increased. (b) A surcharge on railway freight on coal coke and limestone was imposed. (c) Transport bottlenecks caused transportation by sea at a higher cost. (d) There were shortages of raw materials and the firm experienced a sharp increase in the wage cost.

In the early phases of the study period the profit margins were under pressure. But profits kept pace with sales later due to the better capacity utilization of the plants. The company showed alround efficiency at the operational level.

C.2.26 Unichem Laboratories Ltd.

The company was started in 1962 at Bombay. It manufactures and deals in chemicals, pharmaceuticals and medicine, The company's products are sold under the brand name 'Unichem'.

Though sales showed an upward trend for much of the time period under study the profit margins remained under pressure. This affected the stock prices and the market value of the firm adversely. However, the firm maintained its growth and expansion policy. The growth was along the following lines. (a) New independent veterinary division was started as a measure of diversification. (b) Some new product lines were launched, viz., depromedrol, calbloc, and nonphin ambosian. (c) The company had entered into a licence agreement with the National Research development Corporation of India for the exclusive rights to manufacture certain products, viz., vitamins and minerals, fortified composite protein foods and xyxyle- resorcin. (d) The comapny started manufacturing and sale of formulations and high technology based products of UPJOHN of USA.

The company had some problems. In particular, (a) The recessionary and inflationary trends in the economy caused some hardships. (b) There were increases in the cost of raw materials, excise duty and other service costs. (c) Shortage of raw materials, water and power cuts continued. (d) Labor trouble was persistent. (e) The payroll expenses, repair and modernisation expenses also caused problems.

Despite such problems the company maintained a high volume of sales and exported its products to U.K., Russia and CIS markets.

C.2.27 Union Carbide India Ltd.

Union Carbide was incorporated as a private limited company in 1934 and was converted into a public limited company in 1955. It produces consumer products, chemicals and plastics, carbon, metals, and marine and agricultural products. The company uses the brand name 'Eveready', 'National', 'Natex', and 'Union Carbide'.

The company paid dividends at a moderate level and almost regularly which shows that the company had preference for internal financing. Throughout the study period there was an increase in the market price of the shares.

The company started its expansion in the following dimensions: (a) set up a facility for processing of 5,000 TPA of marine products. (b) It started manufacturing methabenzthiazuran, propoxur, dry batteries of calcium carbide and acetylene. (c) The company received the permission to engage in exports of computer and software service. (d) Trawling for deep sea lobster was started off the western continental shelf.

Despite the depressed level of economic activity during 1970s the company had good demand for its product. The battery plant continued to work multiple shifts throughout the year. The sales of organic chemicals and plastics were generally depressed. The marine and agriculture products showed better performance. The company exported batteries and shrimps to the western hemisphere at an increasing level. But the profits were not commensurate with the sales. The chemical and plastic unit was purchsed by Oswal Agro Mills in 1989. The main cause of lower profitability were (a) labor problem, (b) high price of raw materials and difficulties in obtaining raw material, (c) high interest and depreciation provision, (d) increased competition and sluggish economic conditions, (e) shortage of power, (f) credit squeeze, and (g) the Bhopal disaster.

C.3 Outliers

Initial testing was done with the data assembled. Some observations turned out to be outliers. They were eliminated. No further attempt was made to see what caused then to be outliers or what additional variables can explain such large changes. The basic reasons for this is of course the limitations of the data available.

Most of the firms have a tendency to depend on the current and expected market conditions while determining the new investments and the rate of growth of capital assets. It is therefore possible that the GRTH variable exhibits large and sometimes difficult to explain changes. The problem is compounded by the fact that current information reflected in the balance sheet and/or the profit and loss account does not have an adequate explanation for the growth choices of the firms. In general, it was found that the variables used in the present study offer only a partial explanation of the variability of the GRTH variable. Large changes in GRTH are outliers in the present modelling framework. Some observations had to be deleted after initial experimentation. The financing decision is, in a sense, derived from growth decisions and the general perference to finance capital assets by debt initially. The outliers in the DEBT variables are, in many cases, the outliers in the growth time series. Even in those cases where the DEBT variables is away from the average the variables used in the model provided an adequate explanation. As such there were not many outliers in the time series for DEBT. It was not a necessary to eliminate observations just because the DEBT variable is too large or too small. The preference of most firms is debt financing in the initial stages which was converted into equity financing once the initial uncertainties of the new capital projects were resolved.

Glossary

Adverse Selection. One of the parties in a contract experiences information asymmetry. The better informed party can utilize this to influence the terms of the contract in its favour.

Agency Problem. The problem that arises when managers (agents) pursue their own goals, even if that entails lower profits for the owners of the firms (principals).

Agency Cost. The cost borne by the principal to restrict the opportunistic behaviour of the management. It is the total sum of monitoring cost incurred by the principal, the bonding expenditures by the agents and residual loss.

Bonding Cost. The expenditures by the agent to guarantee that he will not take certain actions which would harm the principal.

Book Value. It is the amount of net assets that would be available per equity share, after company pays off all liabilities including preference shares from the sale proceeds of all its assets liquidated at balance sheet values.

Business Risk. Business risk as the variability in the earnings of the firm resulting from the uncertainty in the demand for the products of the firm.

Cadbury Committee. recommended that it is necessary to keep the roles of the chairman and the CEO (Chief Executive Officer) seperate if the shareholders wish to retain an effective control.

Capital Assets. are assets of various kinds including land, building and shares etc.

Capital Gain. The profit on a capital asset, being the excess of selling price over the purchase cost.

Capital Market. is that segment of the financial markets in which securities having maturities exceeding one year are traded.

Capital Structure. Debt/Equity Ratio or the mix of long term sources of funds of a company consisting of term loans, bonds, preference shares, equity shares and reserves.

Corporate Control, includes the power to exercise discretion over major decisions making.

Debenture. A debt security issued by companies, having a certain maturity and bearing a stated coupan rate.

Debt. The firm's obligations in the from of bonds and short term borrowings.

Distinctive Competence. is a firm's ability to complete an action in a manner superior to that of its competitors or to apply a skill that competitors lack. Such distinctive competencies can be found in functional areas, e.g., personnel, production, marketing, finance, and so on.

Diversification, refers to a policy of spreading the range of products marketed and has the analogous motive of reducing reliance upon the vagaries of the markets of a small number of products.

Diversifiable Risk. Risk that can be eliminated by diversification e.g., by investing in many projects.

Dividend. The payment made by a company to its shareholders.

Economies of Scale. When a firm's cost is less than double in response to a doubling of output.

Economies of Scope. Economies of producing multiple goods or services. Thus economies of scope exist if it is cheaper to produce both goods X and goods Y together rather than separately.

Efficiency. The use of economic resources that produces the maximum level of satisfaction possible with the given inputs and technology.

Equity Capital. Funds supplied by the owners of a business. Such an investment yield a share in ownership along with the corresponding risk of loss and the chance of profit.

Financial Risk. The chance that a firm may not be able to meet its financial obligations. Firms that have a high level of debt are subject to greater financial risk.

Governance Mechanism. A centralized decision process in the hands of the board of directors. The management is expected to implement the decisions made by the board of directors.

Implicit Contract. Decision power delegated to the management with a supervisory role assigned to the board of directors.

Information Asymmetry. A situation in which the two parties of a contract have different information about the transaction.

Internal Capital Market. In this system the profit generating divisions remit cash to corporate headquarters which then reallocates investment funds back to finance divisional projects.

Liability. A claim against a company or an individual

acknowledges as due. Examples of liabilities are bills payable, accrued wages, bank loans and debentures. 'Short-term' liabilities to be paid within a year, e.g., salaries and taxes due, whereas 'Long-term' liabilities such as mortgages and bonds run for periods exceeding one year.

Limited Liability. The restrictions of an owner's loss in a business to the amount of capital that owner has contributed to the company. The limitation allows people to invest in a corporation without fear of losing all their personal assets.

M-form Organization. A common type of internal organization adopted by large corporations in response to managerial slack. Responsibility for production activities is decentralized by the formation of operating divisions, each of which possess their own managerial structures. Decisions on capital allocation are centralized, in that they are undertaken by higher level executives generally have an equity stake in the corporation and, therefore, have an incentive to use their control over the flow of capital to sanction those operating divisions whose profitability is unsatisfactory.

Market Value of the Firm. The market value of the firm represents the expected value of the capital assets of the firm at any given point of time.

MAVA = Market value of the firm (Rs. crores)
= (valuation ratio)* (book value of common stock)+ preference capital + long term loans + debentures

where, valuation ratio = market price/book value of a unit of common stock

Monitoring Cost. The principal can limit the discretionary behaviour of the management that create divergences from his interest by establishing incentives, auditing financial statements, etc. The cost incurred by the principal in the above form is called monitoring cost.

Moral Hazard. Behavior of at least one party in a contract is unobservable ex post. Such behavior can have an influence on the payoffs to both parties. In such cases there is always a potential for the party who has the information advantage to modify its behavior to the detriment of the welfare of the other.

Preference Capital. A share that bears a stated dividend and has priority of claim over equity shares in the matter of dividend, assets in the event of liquidation of the company.

Reserves. The amount of profits after taxes not paid out as dividends, which is, therefore, available to a company to finance additional assets. Thus, reserves form a part of net worth which represents the total funds belonging to shareholders.

Risk. A context in which an event occurs with some probability. The risk of an investment refers to the variability of its rate of return.

Separation of ownership and control. A characteristic of most large corporations today. They are owned by their shareholders but operated and conducted by their professional managers. In such situations, actual control exercised by the shareholders is negligible.

Takeover. The acquisition by a raider company of more than 51% of the voting shares of another company.

Transaction Cost. The costs other than price incurred in trading goods and services.

Index